Best Easy Day Hikes Series

Best Easy Day Hikes
Moab

Stewart M. Green

FALCONGUIDES

GUILFORD, CONNECTICUT
HELENA, MONTANA

AN IMPRINT OF GLOBE PEQUOT PRESS

FALCONGUIDES®

Copyright © 2011 by Morris Book Publishing, LLC

FalconGuides is an imprint of Globe Pequot Press.
Falcon, FalconGuides, and Outfit Your Mind are registered trademarks of Morris Book Publishing, LLC.

TOPO! Explorer software and SuperQuad source maps courtesy of National Geographic Maps. For information about TOPO! Explorer, TOPO!, and Nat Geo Maps products, go to www.topo.com or www.natgeomaps.com.

Layout: Kevin Mak
Project editor: Gregory Hyman
Maps by Trailhead Graphics Inc. © Morris Book Publishing, LLC

Library of Congress Cataloging-in-Publication data is available on file.

ISBN 978-0-7627-6358-0

Printed in the United States of America

Contents

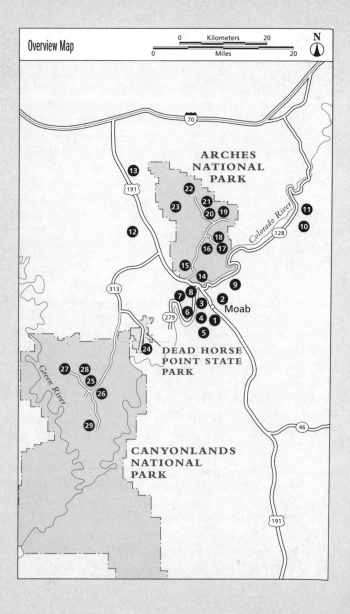

Overview Map

Kilometers
0   20

Miles
0   20

N

ARCHES NATIONAL PARK

Colorado River

Moab

DEAD HORSE POINT STATE PARK

Green River

CANYONLANDS NATIONAL PARK

Introduction

Moab—there's a lot of magic in that name. It conjures up bare-bones landscapes of stunning beauty, deep canyons excavated by the Colorado River, distant vistas of peak and plain, long cliff bands of multicolored sandstone, and soaring towers and arches that scrape against the blue sky. The Moab area, with its vast uninhabited tracts of sandstone canyons, cliffs, and mesas, is an outdoor paradise for hikers.

The Moab area, including the Colorado River canyons, Arches National Park, and Canyonlands National Park, offers lots of excellent trails that thread through canyons, climb mesas and buttes, and traverse sand dunes and slick-rock. *Best Easy Day Hikes Moab* describes twenty-nine of the best hikes and trails for the casual hiker within 40 miles of the town.

If you are on a tight schedule or want to do a short, fun hike in a scenic area, the hikes in this book, hand-picked by the author, allow you to quickly select a day hike suited to your abilities and time constraints. Most of the hikes are between 1 and 3 miles long, although some are shorter and some are longer. Also included are easy strolls and nature walks for families and barrier-free trails that are wheelchair accessible. All the trailheads are easily reached by auto and have parking lots, and some have facilities, including water and toilets. The hikes are also rated by difficulty from easiest to more challenging. Check the listing to help you decide which hike is best for you and your party.

One of the best ways to enjoy, understand, and appreciate the red rock canyon country is by hiking over its diverse terrain. Footpaths take you away from highways and roads and into ancient landscapes preserved in the dry desert air, up hidden canyons filled with sunlight and birdsong, under shining cliffs to arching sweeps of sandstone, and to scenic overlooks with views that reach distant horizons. Every hiker interested in the varied ecosystems found in the Moab region, which range from lush riparian zones along the Colorado River and in deep canyons with perennial streams to austere gardens of juniper, yucca, and Indian paintbrush tucked in slickrock hollows, can learn much by hiking Moab's many trails.

Best Easy Day Hikes Moab is about walking for pleasure—about the joy of putting on boots, filling up a water bottle, shouldering a pack, and setting off into the world. Pick an easy trail and follow your feet. You'll find you can go just about anywhere.

Leave No Trace

Trails in the Moab area are heavily used year-round. We, as trail users and advocates, must be especially vigilant to make sure our passage leaves no lasting mark. Here are some basic guidelines for preserving trails in the region:

- Be prepared. Bring or wear clothes to protect you from cold, heat, or rain. Use maps to navigate (and do not rely solely on the maps included in this book).

- Avoid damaging trailside soils and plants by remaining on the established route. This is also a good rule of thumb for avoiding trailside irritants, like poison ivy.

- Pack out all your own trash, including biodegradable items like orange peels. You might also pack out garbage left by less considerate hikers. Use outhouses at trailheads or along the trail, and keep water sources clean.

- Don't pick wildflowers or gather rocks, antlers, feathers, and other treasures along the trail. Removing these items will only take away from the next hiker's experience.

- Don't approach or feed any wild creatures—the ground squirrel eyeing your snack food is best able to survive if it remains self-reliant. Control pets at all times.

- Be kind to other visitors. Be courteous by not making loud noises while hiking and be aware that you share the trail with others. Yield to other trail users when appropriate.

Desert Dangers

The canyon country surrounding Moab is filled with objective hazards and dangers. Always be aware of your surroundings to keep your children, your friends, and yourself safe when you're hiking in the backcountry.

Falling is the greatest danger and the leading cause of accidents and deaths in the canyon country. Cliffs are everywhere and most, composed of different kinds of sandstone, are loose and friable. Cliff edges can break off, causing you to fall and fracture a leg or worse. A fall of only twenty feet can be fatal. You can also slip and fall on loose boulders.

Avoid climbing on cliffs or traversing across ledges on cliff faces without climbing equipment and the knowledge to use it safely. Restrain your children and keep them away from cliff edges. Unfenced overlooks above cliffs as high as 500 feet are everywhere on these easy hikes, including popular trails like Delicate Arch, Mesa Arch, Upheaval Dome, Grand View Point, and Dead Horse Point.

Watch your footing, especially on uneven terrain, loose boulders, and slickrock coated with snow, water, or sand.

Wear shoes with rubber soles rather than leather. Be aware of drop-offs when taking photographs.

Some trails travel across slickrock terrain or up washes susceptible to flash floods, which can wash the trail away. Most of the trails that cross bare rock are well marked with cairns or small rock piles. Navigate across the area by hiking from cairn to cairn. The good thing here is that there is little vegetation, so if you pay attention to your surroundings and landmarks, you can navigate back to the trailhead.

If you do get lost or become disoriented, don't panic. Instead, sit down in a shady spot and try to figure out where you are. Look for bearings, landmarks, and your footprints. Check the map in this guide. Listen for other hikers or the sound of distant cars on a road. You can also get cell phone reception on most of the trails in this book, especially if you climb on top of a higher ridge and get out of the canyon bottoms. Call 911 or the Grand County Search and Rescue. They're skilled at finding you and getting you out safely.

Be Prepared

Hiking, though immensely rewarding, also comes with hazards and inherent risks, especially for those who arrive unprepared. Respect the desert environment and be prepared for emergency situations and you'll be safe. Remember that many dangers are found in the desert area surrounding Moab.

You must assume responsibility for your own actions and for your safety. Be aware of your surroundings and of dangers, including drop-offs, cliffs, and loose rock; the weather; and the physical condition of both your party and yourself. Never be afraid to turn around if conditions aren't right. Pay attention to those bad feelings—they keep you alive.

Here are a few suggestions to help you prepare for emergency situations on your hike:

Bring a raincoat, even in summer. The afternoon weather can change in an instant. Heavy thunderstorms occur on summer afternoons. In the event of rain, get out of canyons and washes and climb to higher ground. Flash floods regularly occur.

Desert thunderstorms are always accompanied by lightning strikes. Pay attention to the weather and get off high places, including mesas, buttes, and ridge lines before a storm arrives. If you can hear thunder, you're probably not safe.

The air is thin and the sun is bright. Summer temperatures are usually hot; 100 degrees is not uncommon. Use sunscreen on all visible body parts to avoid damaging sunburns and wear a hat to shade and cool your head. Lip block keeps your lips from getting painfully chapped in the dry air. Reapply regularly. Insect repellent is a good idea in summer to ward off biting gnats, flies, and mosquitoes.

Carry plenty of water and sports drinks for electrolyte replacement due to sweating. Don't drink any water from streams unless you treat and purify it. Bring at least a gallon of liquid per person per day during the hotter months from May through September. People die of dehydration, heat exhaustion, and sunstroke here.

Allow enough time for your hike. If you start in late afternoon, bring a headlamp or flashlight so you can see the trail in the dark.

Bring plenty of high-energy snacks for the trail and treats for the youngsters.

Wear comfortable hiking shoes and good socks. Your feet will thank you for that. To avoid blisters, break in your shoes before wearing them in the backcountry.

Enjoy wildlife you see along the trail, but keep your distance and treat the animals with respect. Most critters here do one of three things—bite, stab, or sting. Cute little animals can bite and spread diseases like rabies. Rattlesnakes are found but most are shy and retiring. Watch where you place your hands and feet. Don't feed wildlife to avoid disrupting their natural eating habits. Keep dogs under control so they don't bother wildlife.

Protect and conserve desert water sources, including potholes filled with rainwater and pools in canyons. Water is scarce here and wildlife needs it to survive. Camp at least 300 feet from water sources to allow wildlife access. Try to always carry your own water rather than purifying existing sources. Don't disturb water in potholes, which are often the only water source found for miles. Don't bathe or wash in potholes, wells, or springs.

Carry a day pack to tote all your trail needs, including raincoat, food, water, first-aid kit, flashlight, matches, and extra clothes. A whistle, GPS unit, topo map, binoculars, camera, pocketknife, and FalconGuide identification books for plants, animals, tracks, and scat are all handy additions. And don't forget your *Best Easy Day Hikes Moab* book!

Trail Finder

Best Hikes for Solitude

Map Legend

Transportation

🛣 **70** Interstate
🛣 **191** U.S. Highway
🛣 **128** State Highway
── Other Road
═ ═ ═ ═ Unpaved Road
├──┼──┤ Railroad

Trails

▪▬▪▬▪ Featured Trail
─ ─ ─ ─ Trail
──── Paved Trail/Bike Path
→ Direction of Route

Water/Land Features

▬▬▬ Large River
～～ River/Creek
─··─··─ Intermittent Stream

Symbols

⩃ Bridge
▲ Campground
▲ Mountain/Peak
🅿 Parking
🚉 Picnic Area
■ Point of Interest
🚻 Restroom
○ Town
12 Trailhead
⬗ Viewpoint/Overlook

Land Management

▭ National Park
▭ State Park/Wilderness Study Area

1 Hidden Valley Trail

A steep hike leads to a hidden valley high above Moab and Spanish Valley. After climbing quickly to the valley, the trail traverses it below gorgeous, towering cliffs.

Distance: 4 miles out and back
Approximate hiking time: 2 to 3 hours
Difficulty: More challenging due to 680-foot elevation gain
Trail surface: Single-track dirt trail
Best season: Year-round; summers are hot.
Other trail users: Occasional mountain bikers

Canine compatibility: Dogs allowed on leash
Fees and permits: No fee
Maps: USGS Moab, *Moab Trails Illustrated Explorer*
Trail contacts: Bureau of Land Management (BLM), Moab Field Office, 82 E. Dogwood, Moab 84532; (435) 259-2100; www .blm.gov/ut/st/en/fo/moab.html

Finding the trailhead: From Moab, drive 3 miles south on US 191 and turn right (west) on Angel Rock Road. Drive 2 blocks and turn right on Rimrock Road. Drive to the parking area and trailhead at the road's end. GPS: N 38 31.896' / W 109 31.036'

The Hike

The Hidden Valley Trail, a wonderful adventure hike in the cliffs directly south of Moab, is a trail of two faces. The first trail section is rough, rocky, and difficult, sharply climbing almost 600 feet in its first 0.6 mile. Above that the single-track trail enters Hidden Valley and levels out with gradual grades and an even dirt surface. Take your time on the uphill and you'll be rewarded with scenic views, solitude, and a fine rock art panel.

The trail is hot during the warm months. Hike during the afternoon when the lower part of the trail lies in the shade of the cliffs above. Bring plenty of water, use sunscreen, and wear a hat. Little shade is found along the trail. Watch for occasional mountain bikers who descend the trail, although they have to carry their bikes down the steep section.

The trailhead is on the south side of the dirt parking area on the south side of Spanish Valley a few miles south of Moab. A BLM map at the trailhead includes a short trail description and information about cryptobiotic soil and minimum-impact practices.

Hike south on the trail up an outwash slope to a BLM register box. Sign in and continue up the trail, switchbacking up steep boulder-strewn slopes and dipping across dry washes. After 0.5 mile the trail begins to flatten out and enters the eastern end of Hidden Valley.

Hidden Valley is exactly that, a wide, shallow valley that is hidden from view. Low cliffs hem it on the north while a towering escarpment of sandstone cliffs, capped by rounded domes composed of Navajo Sandstone, form the southern rim of the valley. The valley's flat sandy floor is covered with grass and scattered juniper trees.

The trail gently rises up the valley and after 1.2 miles reaches a low divide. Hike another 0.8 mile to the western end of the valley and climb a short hill to a saddle and the turnaround point for the hike. You'll find great views of Hidden Valley to the east and cliffs, fins, and domes to the south and west. This part of Hidden Valley as well as the surrounding area is part of 12,635-acre Behind the Rocks Wilderness Study Area. To finish the described hike, simply retrace your steps to the trailhead.

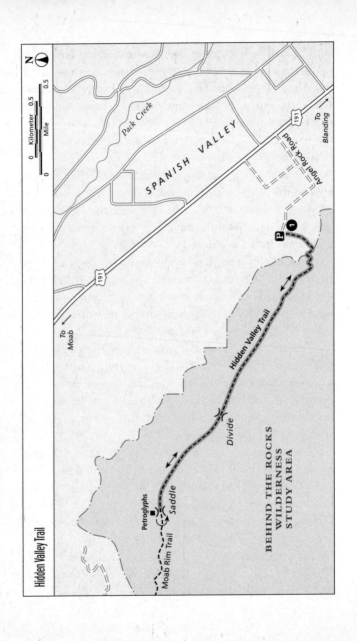

Hidden Valley Trail

N

0   0.5   Kilometer
0   0.5   Mile

Pack Creek

SPANISH VALLEY

191

Angel Rock road

191

To Blanding

To Moab

P
1

Hidden Valley Trail

Divide

Saddle

Petroglyphs

Moab Rim Trail

BEHIND THE ROCKS
WILDERNESS
STUDY AREA

Options: The Hidden Valley Trail follows an ancient path used by Native Americans for the past two thousand years. An optional well-used trail provides evidence of their passage in a petroglyph panel at the base of nearby cliffs to the west. To find the rock art, follow the trail that begins at the saddle and goes west on the north side of a cliff band then scrambles up to the cliff base. Go left from the prow of the cliff to find the petroglyphs. Then return to the saddle and follow the Hidden Valley Trail back to the trailhead. It's downhill all the way.

Or, for extra credit and more miles, you can continue west from the saddle on Hidden Valley Trail, which descends 0.3 mile to the Moab Rim Trail, a four-wheel-drive track that steeply descends another 3 miles to the Colorado River and Kane Creek Road. You need to have a vehicle parked at the western terminus so you can return to the Hidden Valley trailhead and your vehicle.

Miles and Directions

- **0.0** Begin at the trailhead.
- **0.1** Arrive at the BLM register box.
- **0.6** Reach the eastern end of Hidden Valley.
- **1.2** Reach the divide in Hidden Valley.
- **2.0** The trail ends at a saddle. Retrace your steps toward the trailhead.
- **4.0** Arrive back at the trailhead.

2 Mill Creek Trail

Enjoy views of a spectacular cliff-lined canyon on this easy hike along a perennial creek. The hike ends below a couple of popular swimming holes.

Distance: 1.4 miles out and back

Approximate hiking time: 30 minutes to 1 hour

Difficulty: Easy; minimal elevation gain

Trail surface: Single-track dirt path

Best season: Year-round. Best months are April to October.

Other trail users: None

Canine compatibility: Dogs allowed

Fees and permits: No fee

Maps: USGS Moab, *Moab Trails Illustrated Explorer*

Trail contacts: Bureau of Land Management (BLM), Moab Field Office, 82 E. Dogwood, Moab 84532; (435) 259-2100; www .blm.gov/ut/st/en/fo/moab.html

Finding the trailhead: From US 191 in downtown Moab, turn east on Center Street and drive to 400 E. Turn right on 400 E. and drive to Mill Creek Drive. Turn left and follow Mill Creek Drive east to its junction with Sand Flats Road and angle right on Mill Creek Road to Powerhouse Lane after 0.4 mile. Turn left (east) on Powerhouse Lane and drive to its end at a large parking area and the trailhead. GPS: N 38 30.609' / W 109 35.833'

The Hike

The Mill Creek Trail follows Mill Creek, a perennial stream that begins high in the La Sal Mountains, through a deep sandstone canyon east of Moab. The described easy hike follows the trail for 0.7 mile to the fork between Mill Creek and the North Fork of Mill Creek.

Mill Creek Trail, like all Moab canyon hikes, is susceptible to flash flooding, particularly in July and August. Watch the weather and get out of the canyon during thunderstorms. Mill Creek drains a large area and any heavy rain upstream can cause flooding. In the event of flooding, climb to higher ground. Also avoid poison ivy.

The hike begins at the trailhead at a large parking area at the eastern end of Powerhouse Lane, a short drive east of downtown Moab. A BLM sign with Mill Creek information and regulations marks the trail's start. The wide dirt trail gently descends east. A hundred yards down the trail is a small building and a junction with Mill Creek Rim Trail, which heads right and climbs onto the canyon rim to the south. Keep left on the main trail.

After 0.2 mile you reach the ruins on an old dam that generated electrical power for Moab beginning in 1919, when a concrete dam was built. An earlier wooden dam was destroyed by a flash flood in August 1919. The station provided power to Moab until a power line was built from Price to Moab in 1945. Below the dam, Mill Creek dashes through a shallow rock-walled canyon toward Moab. This creek section is a popular wading spot in summer.

Keep right at the dam and walk across rock ledges above the right side of the creek. Large pools built by beavers form upstream from the dam. If you're hiking with a dog, restrain it since beavers will attack dogs that swim in their ponds. Follow the trail through brush, then emerge onto a sandy bench. After 0.5 mile the canyon begins to narrow. A huge tawny wall of Navajo Sandstone looms to the left, lording over the lower canyon. The trail hugs the right side of the canyon and after 0.7 mile reaches the junction of Mill Creek and its north fork. This is a good turnaround point for easy day hikers.

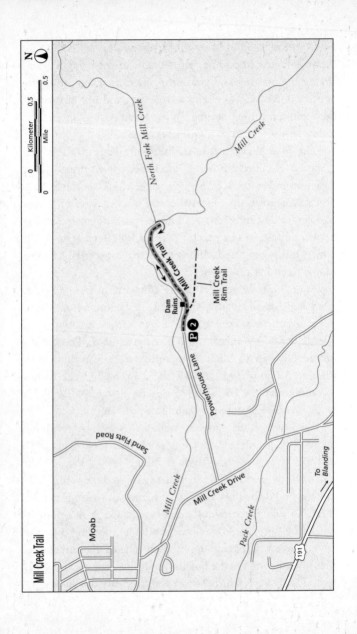

Options: It is well worth your time and effort to explore farther up either fork. Both trails are easily accessible and very popular in the warmer months, with scenic views, rock art panels, and swimming holes. These trails cross the stream several times, requiring you to wade or hop across slippery boulders, which can be difficult from November to April because the water is cold and can be deep at the fords. Best to hike when it's warm so you can wear sandals for the crossings and can plan to get wet. Pools that are deep enough for swimming are found in both forks, although flooding can alter the depth. Avoid jumping from cliffs into the pools. Serious injuries have occurred here from cliff jumping.

The north fork, in particular (to the left and called Left Hand by locals), offers an excellent adventure. The canyon pinches down above the fork. Hike up it for 0.4 mile to a large popular swimming hole below a waterfall. Another pool is another half mile up the canyon. Look for rock art panels about 500 feet before the first pool, between the two pools, and 500 feet past the second pool.

Miles and Directions

0.0   Begin at the trailhead.

0.2   Arrive at the dam ruins.

0.7   Reach the junction of Mill Creek and North Fork. This is the turnaround point.

1.4   Return to the trailhead.

3 Scott M. Matheson Wetlands Preserve Trail

This trail west of Moab wanders through a riparian wetland with shady trees, meadows, and lots of wildlife on the Colorado River floodplain.

Distance: 1-mile loop
Approximate hiking time: 30 minutes to 1 hour
Difficulty: Easy; minimal elevation loss and gain
Trail surface: Double-track compacted dirt path (wheelchair accessible)
Best season: Year-round
Other trail users: None

Canine compatibility: No dogs allowed
Fees and permits: No fee
Maps: USGS Moab, *Moab Trails Illustrated Explorer*
Trail contacts: The Nature Conservancy, Moab Project Office, P.O. Box 1329, 820 Kane Creek Blvd., Moab 84532; (435) 259-4629; www.nature.org

Finding the trailhead: From Main Street (US 191) on the south side of Moab, turn west on Kane Creek Boulevard at the McDonald's restaurant and drive west to a Y-junction with 500 West. Keep left on the paved road and follow it to the signed trailhead on the right, 0.9 mile from US 191. GPS: N 38 34.399' / W 109 34.265'

The Hike

This hike makes a mile-long loop through the 890-acre Scott M. Matheson Wetlands Preserve along the Colorado River west of Moab. The area, administered by The Nature Conservancy, preserves the lush bottomlands of the river and forms a counterpoint oasis to the surrounding stone landscape. This riparian wetland, the most species-rich habitat in southeastern Utah, attracts lots of wildlife, including over 225 bird species, northern leopard frogs, mule deer, raccoons, beaver, muskrat, and foxes. The area is locally called the Moab Sloughs.

The easy hike, following a broad compacted-dirt trail, explores the southern part of the preserve. Benches and a covered wildlife blind allow you to stop and observe animals and birds or to soak up the quiet. The trail makes a good shady alternative on hot days. Bring water, sunscreen, a hat, and mosquito repellent in summer.

The trailhead is at the north side of the preserve's parking lot just off Kane Springs Road west of US 191 and Moab. A two-panel kiosk welcomes you to this unique natural area and dedicates the preserve to former Utah governor Scott M. Matheson, who died in 1990. Walk north on the wide path and cross a bridge which arcs over Mill Creek. At 0.1 mile on the other side of the bridge is a five-panel interpretative display about land, water, life, worth, and people. Take a moment to read the signs before continuing your hike.

Just past the information kiosk is a trail junction with a preserve map. Go right and follow the trail beneath cottonwood and black willow trees. After 0.2 mile you'll come to a trail junction. Go right on a 0.1-mile spur, which leads to an elevated boardwalk, made with wood from a railroad trestle that once crossed part of the Great Salt Lake, across a marshy area. End at an octagonal wildlife observation blind with a roof and open windows. This is a good spot to get your binoculars out and spot some birds.

From the blind, return south to the trail junction and go right (west). This next 0.5-mile trail segment heads west to

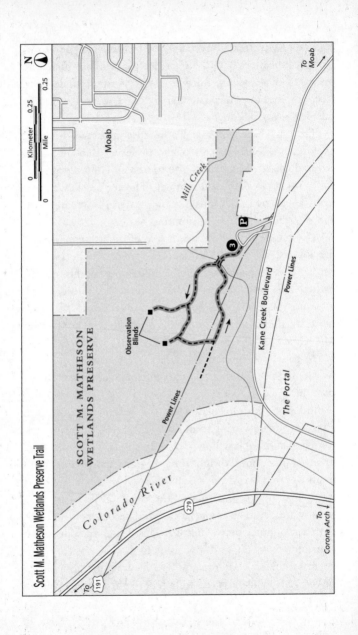

Scott M. Matheson Wetlands Preserve Trail

SCOTT M. MATHESON
WETLANDS PRESERVE

Observation
Blinds

Colorado River

Mill Creek

Moab

To
Moab

To
191

To
Corona Arch

Kane Creek Boulevard

The Portal

Power Lines

Power Lines

Power Lines

279

N

Kilometer
0   0.25

Mile
0   0.25

P

3

a long boardwalk. A short spur leads to an observation platform. Continue on the boardwalk, which bends south and then makes a sharp turn left (east). At this turn is another trail junction. The main trail goes left, but a narrow single-track spur path heads right or west through open meadows toward the Colorado River.

At the junction, go left and hike along the south edge of dense forest and below power lines. The trail bends left and reenters the shady woods, passing open grassy glades, and after 0.9 mile reaches the original trail junction and kiosk. Go right and cross the Mill Creek bridge to return to the trailhead.

Miles and Directions

0.0 Begin at the trailhead.

0.1 Pass the interpretive display and arrive at a trail junction. Go right.

0.2 Reach a trail junction with the first spur trail to an observation hut. Go right 0.1 mile to the hut and return to the trail. Turn right.

0.5 Reach the third trail junction. Go left. The spur path on the right leads toward river.

0.9 Return to the trail junction at the map. Go right to Mill Creek.

1.0 Return to the trailhead.

4 Moonflower Canyon Trail

This short hike, beginning near the Colorado River, leads up a shady, cliff-lined box canyon to a reflecting pool of water at the canyon's end.

Distance: 0.8 mile out and back
Approximate hiking time: 30 minutes
Difficulty: Easy; minimal elevation gain
Trail surface: Single-track dirt path
Best season: Year-round
Other trail users: None

Canine compatibility: Dogs allowed on leash
Fees and permits: No fee
Maps: USGS Moab, *Moab Trails Illustrated Explorer*
Trail contacts: Bureau of Land Management (BLM), Moab Field Office, 82 E. Dogwood, Moab 84532; (435) 259-2100; www .blm.gov/ut/st/en/fo/moab.html

Finding the trailhead: From Main Street (US 191) on the south side of Moab, turn west on Kane Creek Boulevard at the McDonald's restaurant and drive west to a Y-junction with 500 W. Keep left on the paved road, which becomes Kane Springs Road. Follow it for 2.3 miles, bending south along the Colorado River, to a large parking area on the left (east) side of the road for a BLM campground, a petroglyph panel, and the trailhead at the mouth of Moonflower Canyon. GPS: N 38 33.2615' / W 109 5.206'

The Hike

The short Moonflower Canyon Trail explores a box canyon on the east side of the Colorado River just south of Moab. The trail threads up the narrow canyon, passing eight primitive campsites, until it ends at a cul-de-sac below steep Navajo sandstone cliffs. The canyon floor is shaded by tall cottonwoods. Water flows in the canyon after rain, especially at a rock-lined reflecting pool at the canyon's end below a vertical pour-off. The trail is especially good in autumn when the cottonwoods blaze yellow and in summer when they provide welcome shade.

Before you hike, walk across the sandy parking area to a north-facing cliff covered with black desert varnish. A marvelous 100-foot-long gallery of rock art lines the cliff-base, with some probably 2,000 years old. Note the bighorn sheep and other animal motifs as well as a triangular anthropomorphic figure with a headdress in the Barrier Canyon style. Besides the art left by the ancient ones are modern graffiti and names chiseled on the rock. This panel is not only one of the area's most accessible rock art sites but also its most vandalized site.

Start the hike at the trailhead at the Moonflower Canyon Campground sign on the left side of the parking area. Follow the primitive trail up the canyon, along a usually dry wash beneath tall cottonwood trees and groves of Gambel oak. Towering cliffs loom above as you pass the campsites. The canyon is named for datura, also called moonflowers, a desert plant with white trumpet-shaped flowers. Datura is a sacred plant to Native Americans, who use the plant in ceremonies.

After 0.4 mile you reach the end of the canyon. Large boulders, fallen from the cliffs above, line a spring-fed depression which fills with water when heavy rain drains down sandstone canyons and pours off the cliff above in a 100-foot-high waterfall. It's best to leave the canyon, however, during summer thunderstorms since flash floods can occur.

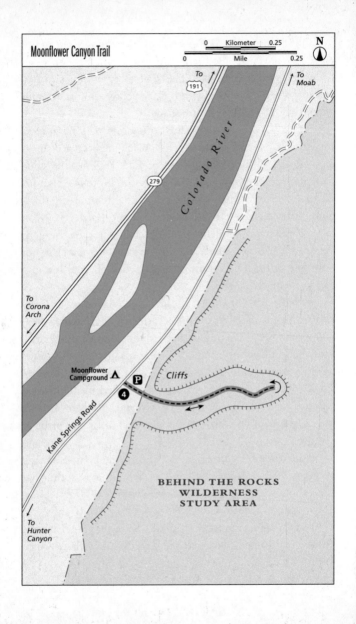

Moonflower Canyon Trail

0 Kilometer 0.25
0 Mile 0.25

N

To 191

To Moab

279

Colorado River

To Corona Arch

Moonflower Campground

P

4

Cliffs

Kane Springs Road

To Hunter Canyon

BEHIND THE ROCKS
WILDERNESS
STUDY AREA

Finish the hike by walking back down the canyon to the trailhead and parking area.

Miles and Directions

0.0 Begin at the trailhead by the Colorado River.

0.4 Reach the end of the canyon and trail. Retrace your steps toward the trailhead.

0.8 Arrive back at the trailhead.

5 Hunter Canyon Trail

This excellent out-and-back trail leads up a canyon lined with towering sandstone cliffs.

Distance: 3.4 miles out and back

Approximate hiking time: 1 to 2 hours

Difficulty: Easy; 250-foot elevation gain

Trail surface: Single-track dirt trail

Best season: Year-round. Summers are hot.

Other trail users: Horses

Canine compatibility: Dogs allowed

Fees and permits: No fee or permit required

Maps: USGS Moab, *Moab Trails Illustrated Explorer*

Trail contacts: Bureau of Land Management (BLM), Moab Field Office, 82 E. Dogwood, Moab 84532; (435) 259-2100; www .blm.gov/ut/st/en/fo/moab.html

---

Finding the trailhead: From Main Street (US 191) on the south side of Moab, turn west on Kane Creek Boulevard at the McDonald's restaurant and drive west to a Y-junction with 500 West. Keep left on the paved road, which becomes Kane Springs Road. Follow the road west and then south along the Colorado River to a cattle guard. Continue south on the narrow dirt road to the signed Hunter Canyon Trailhead on the left just before the road splashes through a creek. This is 7.5 miles from US 191. GPS: N 38 30.596' / W 109 35.794'

The Hike

The Hunter Canyon Trail offers a wonderful out-and-back hike up a deep, twisting canyon lined with towering sandstone cliffs. A small spring-fed creek runs most of the year, pooling in stone basins and cascading over ledges. Dense vegetation, including willow and tamarisk, fills the canyon floor in places but the trail cuts through it. In other spots the creek bed has been rearranged by summer floods, so if you lose the trail or it has been washed out, just continue up the bed and you'll find the trail again.

The hike starts at the junction of Hunter Canyon and Kane Creek Canyon on the left side of Kane Springs Road just before it dips through the creek. The lower part of Hunter Canyon has nine BLM campsites.

Hike east up the sandy trail on the canyon floor, crossing and recrossing the creek whenever needed. The creek is usually low so it's easy to boulder hop across. As in other Moab canyons, flash floods can occur in Hunter Canyon after heavy rainstorms. Watch the weather, especially in July and August, and either turn around or climb to higher ground before flooding occurs.

Tall cottonwoods shade the trail, while thick stands of willow line the creek and groves of scrub oak climb the cooler north-facing slopes below the cliffs. After 0.5 mile the trail follows the creek and bends left below a tall cliff. Opposite the bend is a steep broken drainage. Look up right from the base of the rocky gully to see Hunter Arch, a 74-foot-high opening with a thick outside leg that connects to the rimrock above. If you want to see the arch up close, scramble up the boulder-filled gully and then a steep talus slope to the arch base.

Around the bend from the arch the trail plunges through a dense thicket of tamarisk, an invasive Asian plant, before emerging onto bedrock pavement. The creek trickles through shallow pools on the bedrock. After a mile, the trail and canyon bend eastward. The canyon opens here and three sandstone pinnacles rise above the trail.

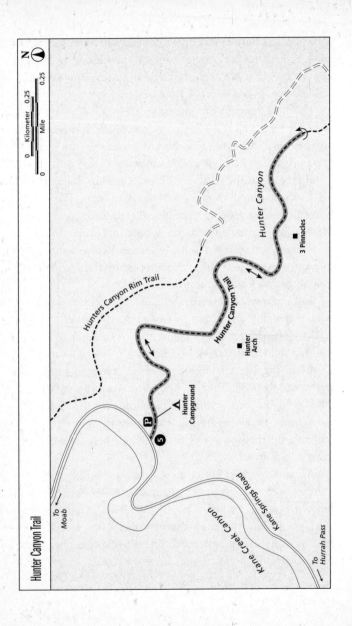

Hunter Canyon Trail

Continue hiking past the left pinnacle into the wider canyon. The creek runs over bedrock. Follow the trail across a sand bench on the left side of the canyon and then go right onto bedrock next to the creek. The creek tumbles over short stone ledges, filling large shallow pools that reflect sky and red cliff.

This idyllic spot, 1.7 miles from the trailhead, is the turnaround point for this easy day hike. It's a good place to bask on the rocks like a lizard or to take off your shoes and soak your tired feet in the creek. To finish your hike, retrace your footsteps back down Hunter Canyon to the trailhead.

Options: The Hunter Canyon Trail continues another half mile or so up around the next bend where the trail ends at a pour-off or dry waterfall that is difficult to pass. The side canyon to the south before the pour-off harbors Curious Arch, a small arch perched on the canyon rim.

Miles and Directions

0.0 Begin at the trailhead on Kane Springs Road.

0.5 Enter the canyon below Hunter Arch.

1.2 Reach the three pinnacles.

1.7 Arrive at the turnaround point on bedrock slabs. Retrace your steps back toward the trailhead.

3.4 Arrive back at the trailhead.

6 Dinosaur Tracks Trail

Families with dinosaur enthusiasts (of all ages) will enjoy this interesting short hike to a large boulder with dinosaur tracks above the Colorado River.

Distance: 0.2 mile out and back
Approximate hiking time: 15 to 30 minutes
Difficulty: Easy; 50-foot elevation gain
Trail surface: Single-track dirt trail
Best season: Year-round
Other trail users: None

Canine compatibility: Dogs allowed on leash
Fees and permits: No fee
Maps: USGS Moab, *Moab Trails Illustrated Explorer*
Trail contacts: Bureau of Land Management (BLM), Moab Field Office, 82 E. Dogwood, Moab 84532; (435) 259-2100; www.blm.gov/ut/st/en/fo/moab.html

Finding the trailhead: From Moab, drive northwest on US 191 to a left (south) turn on UT 279/Potash Road (1.3 miles west of the Colorado River Bridge). Drive south on UT 279 for 6 miles to a right turn to the signed Poison Spider Mesa trailhead for mountain bikes, ATVs, and jeeps. Drive 0.1 mile up the short dirt road to a large parking area with a pit toilet and information kiosk. The Dinosaur Track Trailhead is on the north side of the lot. GPS: N 38 31.973' / W 109 36.521'

The Hike

The Dinosaur Tracks Trail is a short, easy hike to a unique dinosaur trackway on a tilted boulder face above the Colorado River. The site, an open-air museum, offers a unique view into ancient lives that occupied an alien world at this very spot on the planet. Before hiking to the trackway, locate the flat angled rock face that harbors it on the cliff terraces

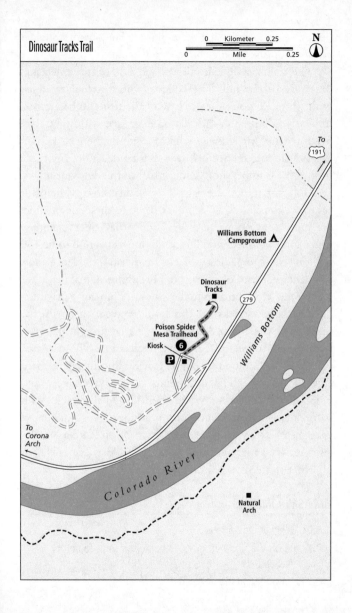

Dinosaur Tracks Trail

0   Kilometer   0.25

0   Mile   0.25

N

To
191

Williams Bottom
Campground

Dinosaur
Tracks

279

Williams Bottom

Poison Spider
Mesa Trailhead

Kiosk   6

P

To
Corona
Arch

Colorado River

Natural
Arch

opposite the pit toilet and the trailhead. The obvious boulder is poised on the skyline above a couple cliff bands.

The trail starts on the right-hand side of the toilets and descends a short hill. The edges of the dirt trail are lined with rocks. As you near the base of the first cliff band, look up and you'll see the dark flat boulder face with the tracks. Scramble up left along a sandstone ramp then back right across a sloping terrace below a cliff band. At the right side of the cliff, climb a short smooth slab to the dinosaur tracks.

Dinosaur tracks, more than any other kind of dinosaur fossil, are the closest we can ever come to these long extinct creatures. If we use our imaginations, they offer a glimpse into a long vanished world from the Jurassic period some 150 million years ago. Dinosaur tracks are dynamic evidence and a momentary record of a living and breathing animal that once stalked the Moab area and offer clues to dinosaur behavior.

The largest tracks on this boulder were made by the three-toed feet of an Allosaurus, a fierce upright predator with dozens of sharp teeth and small arms. The dinosaur walked across a muddy sandbar, leaving imprints of its giant feet, in a lost world with an inland sea, wide rivers, and a dense tropical forest. Water then buried the tracks with sediment, which hardened into sandstone over millions of years before they were exposed by erosion. Other smaller dinosaur tracks are also found on the boulder face as well as on other stone slabs on the hillside.

Miles and Directions

0.0 Begin at the trailhead.
0.1 Reach the dinosaur tracks. Retrace your steps to the trailhead.
0.2 Arrive back at the trailhead.

7 Corona Arch Trail

This excellent hike above the Colorado River Canyon leads to three arches, including Corona Arch, one of the largest arches in the Moab area.

Distance: 3 miles out and back
Approximate hiking time: 2 hours
Difficulty: Moderate; 250-foot elevation gain
Trail surface: Single-track dirt path and sandstone slabs
Best season: Year-round. Summers are hot.
Other trail users: None

Canine compatibility: Dogs allowed
Fees and permits: None
Maps: USGS Gold Bar, *Moab Trails Illustrated Explorer*
Trail contacts: Bureau of Land Management (BLM), Moab Field Office, 82 E. Dogwood, Moab 84532; (435) 259-2100; www .blm.gov/ut/st/en/fo/moab.html

Finding the trailhead: From Moab, drive northwest on US 191 to a left (south) turn on UT 279/Potash Road (1.3 miles west of the Colorado River Bridge). Drive south on UT 279 for 10 miles to the signed Corona Arch Trailhead on the right (east) side of the highway opposite the Gold Bar Campground. GPS: N 38 34.467' / W 109 37.941'

The Hike

The Corona Arch Trail is a great 3-mile hike to one of the largest and most spectacular arches near Moab. Corona Arch, also called Little Rainbow Bridge, is your final destination, but the trail also passes Pinto Arch and Bowtie Arch along the way.

The trail is easy to follow although it does cross some wide expanses of slickrock pavement. These sections, however, are

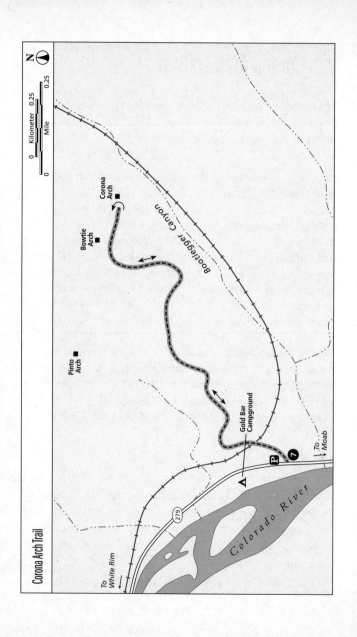

Corona Arch Trail

well marked with cairns. A couple of slickrock sections also have metal cables to use as handrails as well as a ladder on one steep step. If you have a fear of heights or unsure footing, it's best to stop after the first cable to view the arch.

During the warmer months, do this hike first thing in the morning since it gets sun all day. Carry plenty of water and wear a hat. Little shade is found along the trail, except beneath overhanging cliffs in the late afternoon. Watch children, as the trail skirts numerous drop-offs.

Start at the trailhead on the right side of the parking area. The trail quickly climbs a rocky talus slope and reaches a BLM register box just before railroad tracks at 0.1 mile. Sign in and cross the tracks. Trains use the tracks to haul potash from the Potash Mine and North America's largest potash deposit. Potash, used as a water softener and fertilizer, is extracted by solution mining, and then processed and shipped by truck and railroad.

The sandy trail follows an old road north alongside a cliff, then bends right below the cliff. Look up left to the high canyon rim to see Pinto Arch, a pothole arch. The trail climbs up a shallow rocky canyon to a broad bench and heads northeast across sand and slickrock pavement until it's below a tall slabby cliff. Hike across sloping slabs below the cliff to a long cable anchored to posts. Past the cable at 0.7 mile is your first view of Corona Arch, a dramatic span above Bootlegger Canyon. If you're queasy about heights, this is the best turn-around point.

The trail, crossing slickrock pavement, bends left here along a wide stone bench and reaches another cable. Grab the cable and climb steps chopped into a sandstone slab. Climb a five-step metal ladder above to a small, twisted juniper tree and a higher bench. Follow the broad slickrock bench around the head of a cul-de-sac canyon and bend east toward Corona Arch.

Bowtie Arch towers above the trail to your left. This pothole arch formed when a pothole above, usually filled with water, eroded down into a cave below. Continue hiking along a sloping sandstone slab and reach Corona Arch after 1.5 miles.

Corona Arch is a spectacular span composed of Navajo sandstone. The arch opening measures 140 feet across by 105 feet high. Lie down beneath the arch in its long, narrow shadow on hot days to get a true measure of both its size and fragility. Since the arch is located outside of Arches National Park, it hasn't received the same protections as its federally sheltered neighbors, and adventurers use it for fun and excitement. Although the practice is now banned, airplanes have flown through the opening, while climbers still ascend to the top and rappel off.

Finish the hike by following the trail back to the trailhead.

Miles and Directions

0.0 Begin at the trailhead.

0.1 Reach the BLM register box and railroad tracks.

0.7 Ascend to a view of Corona Arch.

1.5 Reach Corona Arch. Reverse your direction here to return to the trailhead.

3.0 Arrive back at the trailhead.

8 Portal Overlook Trail

This strenuous uphill hike leads to a spectacular viewpoint above vertical cliffs overlooking Moab and the Colorado River Canyon.

Distance: 4 miles out and back
Approximate hiking time: 2 to 3 hours
Difficulty: More challenging due to 950-foot elevation gain
Trail surface: Single-track dirt and slickrock trail
Best season: Year-round. Summers are hot.
Other trail users: Mountain bikers

Canine compatibility: Dogs allowed on leash
Fees and permits: No fee or permit
Maps: USGS Moab, *Moab Trails Illustrated Explorer*
Trail contacts: Bureau of Land Management (BLM), Moab Field Office, 82 E. Dogwood, Moab 84532; (435) 259-2100; www .blm.gov/ut/st/en/fo/moab.html

Finding the trailhead: From Moab, drive northwest on US 191 to a left (south) turn on UT 279/Potash Road (1.3 miles west of the Colorado River Bridge). Drive south on UT 279 for 4.2 miles to the Jaycee Park Recreation Site on the right (west) side of the highway. Park in a dirt parking area. The trailhead is on the north (right) side of the lot. GPS: N 38 33.403' / W 109 35.422'

The Hike

The Portal Overlook Trail, while strenuous and mostly uphill, follows a good trail to one of the most spectacular scenic viewpoints in the Moab area. The trail, one of the hardest in this book, is hot in summer but lies in the shade of tall cliffs in the late afternoon. It ends at an unfenced overlook above a 300-foot-high cliff. Watch children on the cliff edge. Mountain bikers also use the trail for a quick descent route from the Poison Spider Mesa trails above.

The trail begins on the right side of the parking lot and right of the BLM sign. Its first half mile parallels the highway and river, passing first beneath shady cottonwoods and then traversing rocky slopes and gravel benches to a register box. Rounded cobbles on the benches, lying atop bedrock sandstone, were deposited by the ancestral Colorado River, which tumbled the rocks down its riverbed from the Colorado Rockies.

After signing into the BLM register at 0.5 mile, continue hiking up the trail which steepens and begins ascending a long inclined ramp composed of gray Kayenta sandstone. Tall cliffs of Navajo sandstone loom above the trail, while cliffs of Wingate sandstone fall away below to the road and river.

The trail slowly ascends the broad Kayenta bench for almost a mile and a half, alternately crossing bare expanses of tilted slickrock pavement and crossing sand and broken boulders. Junipers scatter across the slope. As the trail climbs, the views become more spectacular. To your right is The Portal, a huge cliffed gap that the Colorado River passes through, exiting Spanish Valley and entering a deep canyon.

Finally the Kayenta bench narrows and finally ends above a steep cliff, and after 2 miles of steady uphill hiking you reach the Portal Overlook. This wonderful viewpoint, perched on a sandstone shelf above a 300-foot-high cliff, offers stunning views of the region. Directly below is the muddy Colorado River and The Portal's abrupt cliffs. To the east stretches the long Spanish Valley and the town of Moab. Beyond rises the La Sal Mountains. To the north lie

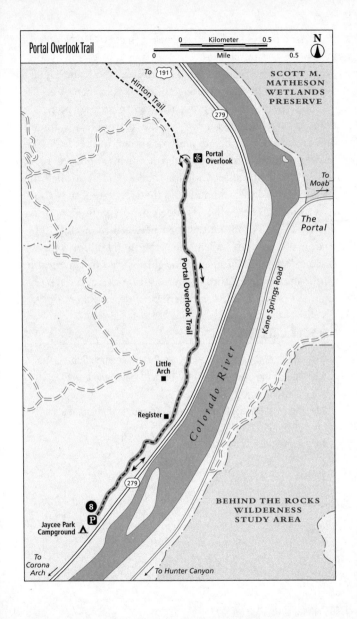

Portal Overlook Trail

0 Kilometer 0.5

0 Mile 0.5

N

SCOTT M.
MATHESON
WETLANDS
PRESERVE

Hinton Trail

To 191

279

To
Moab

Portal
Overlook

The
Portal

Kane Springs Road

Portal Overlook Trail

Colorado River

Little
Arch

Register

BEHIND THE ROCKS
WILDERNESS
STUDY AREA

279

8

P

Jaycee Park
Campground

To
Corona
Arch

To Hunter Canyon

the mesas, buttes, and monuments of Arches National Park. If you look carefully you can spot the tops of the Courthouse Towers, Balanced Rock, Elephant Butte, and Devil's Garden and The Fiery Furnace in the far distance.

This spectacular overlook is the turn-around point for the hike. If you hiked up in the late afternoon, it's a good place to catch your breath and cool down in the shade. To finish the hike, retrace your steps south to the river, road, and trailhead. It's all downhill and takes you about half the time that it did to come up. And the views are just as good.

Options: The Portal Overlook Trail continues across a sloping ledge system sandwiched between high cliffs. This section, sometimes called the Hinton Trail for pioneer rancher William Hinton, was originally used to reach cattle on the mesa above. With dangerous drop-offs and steep terrain, it is only suitable for experienced desert hikers.

Miles and Directions

0.0 Begin at the trailhead at Jaycee Park Recreation Site.

0.5 Reach the BLM register box. The trail leaves the lower canyon.

2.0 Arrive at Portal Overlook and trail's end. From here, retrace your steps to complete the hike.

4.0 Arrive back at the trailhead.

9 Negro Bill Canyon Trail

This excellent hike up lush Negro Bill Canyon leads to a side canyon and Morning Glory Natural Bridge, a spectacular rock formation.

Distance: 4.2 miles out and back

Approximate hiking time: 2 to 3 hours

Difficulty: Moderate; 330-foot elevation gain

Trail surface: Single-track dirt trail

Best season: Year-round. Summers are hot.

Other trail users: None

Canine compatibility: Dogs allowed on leash

Fees and permits: No fee

Maps: USGS Moab, *Moab Trails Illustrated Explorer*

Trail contacts: Bureau of Land Management (BLM), Moab Field Office, 82 E. Dogwood, Moab 84532; (435) 259-2100; www .blm.gov/ut/st/en/fo/moab.html

Finding the trailhead: From Moab, drive north on US 191. Turn right before the Colorado River bridge on UT 128. Drive 3 miles east on UT 128 along the river to the signed trailhead and parking area on the right (south). The trailhead is on the south side of the lot. GPS: N 38 36.592' / W 109 32.012'

The Hike

The 4.2-mile round-trip hike up Negro Bill Canyon to Morning Glory Bridge is simply one of the best easy hikes in the Moab area. The trail has it all—gorgeous scenery with towering Navajo sandstone cliffs, thick vegetation and shade along the canyon floor, a perennial stream that flows year-round, and a dramatic natural bridge, one of the longest stone spans in the United States, at trail's end.

The popular trail is generally easy to follow, with only a few tricky parts where flooding changes the terrain, and crosses the creek many times. If you come on a hot day, wear sandals so you can splash through the water instead of boulder-hopping across the creek. If you're hiking in summer, watch for thunderstorms to the south. Heavy rain can lead to flash flooding in the canyon. Climb to higher ground in case of flood. Poison ivy is found in the canyon, sometimes in dense thickets and especially in the canyon just below Morning Glory Arch. Remember to bring water, sunscreen, and a hat.

Begin the hike at the Negro Bill Trailhead next to a pit toilet on the south side of UT 128/River Road a few miles upstream from Moab. The trail heads south and crosses a sandstone ledge above the creek before dropping to the canyon floor. After 0.3 mile the trail reaches the boundary of the Negro Bill Canyon Wilderness Study Area and a register box.

The canyon's inclusion on the Bureau of Land Management's list of proposed Utah wilderness areas in 1979 led to a local rebellion after the BLM erected a barrier to keep vehicles out of the canyon. Anti-wilderness locals bulldozed the barrier twice before the conflict was resolved in U.S. District Court. Now most of the scars caused by off-road vehicle use have vanished, rehabilitated by water and vegetation.

Continue hiking south on the left side of the creek until you're finally forced to cross it by cliffs. After crossing the creek a couple more times, the canyon and trail reaches a junction with Abyss Canyon, a deep canyon to the right, at 1.1 miles. Keep left here in Negro Bill Canyon and don't make the mistake of hiking up Abyss Canyon. Its primitive trail is rough and brushy.

Hike up a steep section of old road above the right or south side of the creek onto a dry bench. The trail edges across a sandy slope then descends and crosses to the north side of the creek. The canyon is named for William Grandstaff, a black rancher who settled in the Moab area in the late 1870s and grazed cattle in the lush canyon.

After 1.7 miles the trail dips down to the creek and a junction. While a trail continues east up Negro Bill Canyon, go right here up a short side canyon. Note that this is the second side canyon that you reach during the hike.

Splash across the creek, then traverse across steep talus slopes above the densely vegetated canyon to your right. The trail slowly climbs a blunt ridge to a high sandstone bench. Your destination and the trail's end is straight south at the head of the canyon. Follow the bench and after 2.1 miles you reach Morning Glory Bridge, a fitting end to a great hike.

Morning Glory Natural Bridge, the sixth-longest stone span in the United States, vaults 243 feet across the canyon's head. The bridge differs from an arch since it spans a watercourse and was carved by water. During periods when more rain fell here, a spectacular waterfall plunged off the cliff through the 15-foot-wide gap behind the bridge. Now the waterfall flows only after heavy thunderstorms. A natural spring gushes from a crack below the left leg of the arch, giving good drinking water. Watch for dense thickets of poison ivy among the trees and along the trail below the bridge.

After cooling down in the shade of Morning Glory Bridge, follow the trail back north to Negro Bill Canyon. Go left (west) on the main trail and hike west and then north along the creek back to the trailhead.

Miles and Directions

0.0   Begin at the trailhead.
0.3   Enter the Negro Bill Canyon Wilderness Study Area.

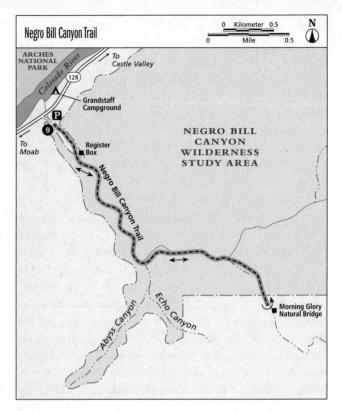

1.1 Reach the junction with Abyss Canyon. Go left into the main canyon.

1.7 Reach a trail junction at the creek fork. Go right or south up the side canyon.

2.1 Arrive at the Morning Glory Natural Bridge and turnaround point.

4.2 Return to the trailhead.

10 Fisher Towers Trail

A maze of soaring sandstone towers surrounds you on this moderate hike to a high ridge above Onion Creek.

Distance: 5.2 miles out and back

Approximate hiking time: 2 to 3 hours

Difficulty: Moderate; 650-foot elevation gain

Trail surface: Single-track dirt and slickrock trail

Best season: Year-round. Summers are hot.

Other trail users: None. Bicycles not allowed.

Canine compatibility: Dogs allowed on leash

Fees and permits: No fee

Maps: USGS Fisher Towers, *Moab Trails Illustrated Explorer*

Trail contacts: Bureau of Land Management (BLM), Moab Field Office, 82 E. Dogwood, Moab 84532; (435) 259-2100; www .blm.gov/ut/st/en/fo/moab.html

Finding the trailhead: Drive north from Moab on US 191 and just before the Colorado River Bridge, turn right (east) onto UT 128/River Road. Follow this paved highway for 21 miles to a turnoff marked Fisher Towers. Turn right (south) and follow a dirt road southeast for another 2 miles to a parking area and campground. GPS: N 38 43.489' / W 109 18.531'

The Hike

The Fisher Towers Trail explores the Fisher Towers, one of the Utah canyon country's most bizarre landscapes. The area is a maze of soaring fins, pinnacles, minarets, gargoyles, spires, and strangely shaped rock formations east of Moab. The towers, soaring monuments to erosion, are composed of dark red Cutler sandstone topped by harder Moenkopi sandstone and draped with mud curtains.

The 2.6-mile trail twists through the towers, dipping into sharp canyons and traversing beneath vertical cliffs, to its far southern terminus, forming a 5.2-mile round-trip hike. You can, however, hike out as far as you want before turning around and retracing your steps back to the trailhead. Many day hikers end their trek at the ridge below Ancient Art, a rock formation with a corkscrew-shaped summit, or at the base of Cottontail Tower's west ridge, one-way hikes of 0.5 and 1.0 mile, respectively.

The single-track Fisher Towers Trail has both a dirt and rock pavement surface. It's easy to follow and is well marked with cairns or rock stacks to point the way. No shade is found on the trail, so plan your hike accordingly on hot days. It's best in the early morning or evening. Remember to bring plenty of water, use sunscreen, and wear a hat.

Begin your Fisher Towers hike at the trailhead and parking lot north of the area. At the trailhead is a trail sign, register, and a pit toilet. Nearby is a small BLM campground. The trail descends a short hill, crosses slickrock, and drops into a canyon. At the bottom, the trail climbs out a side canyon and winds around the west side of Ancient Art. After 0.75 mile the trail reaches a viewpoint south of Ancient Art. A climber's trail goes up left to the spire.

The trail contours into a canyon and then traverses rocky slopes below the north face of looming Cottontail Tower, an 800-foot-high spire. The trail reaches the base of the sharp west ridge of Cottontail after a mile. The bedrock here makes a good resting spot. Lots of hikers turn around here and return to the trailhead.

The next trail segment heads east below the sheer south face of Cottontail on a rock bench before dipping into a canyon. Descend a six-step metal ladder into the canyon,

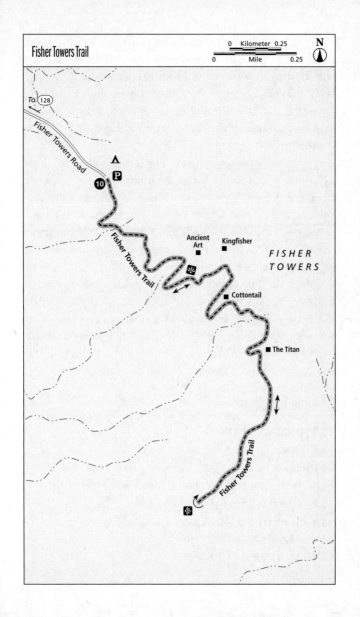

then follow the trail which contours across rocky slopes into another canyon. Past here the trail slowly climbs around The Titan, the tallest of the Fisher Towers and a popular ascent for rock climbers. At 2.0 miles, near the base of The Titan, the trail slips through a stone notch and then edges across an exposed ledge. Watch your footing here if it's wet or snowy.

The trail climbs away from The Titan, following sloping sandstone ledges, and after 2.2 miles climbs onto a high ridge. Enjoy great views of the Fisher Towers and the distant Colorado River Canyon to the north, and to the west a long ridge studded with tall pinnacles including Castleton Tower and The Priest. This is also a good turn-around point if you're tired.

Finish the hike by following the wide sandstone ridge southwest for 0.4 mile, passing above deep canyons which plunge south into Onion Creek's canyon. The trail ends atop a rounded rocky knoll with more fabulous views. After a good rest and drink of water, follow the trail back to the parking area. It goes fast since it's all downhill.

Miles and Directions

- **0.0** Begin at the trailhead.
- **0.5** Reach the ridge below Ancient Art.
- **0.75** Reach the junction with Ancient Art climber's trail.
- **1.0** Arrive at the base of Cottontail Tower's west ridge.
- **2.2** Ascend to the top of the ridge southwest of The Titan.
- **2.6** Reach the end of the trail on a rocky knoll. Retrace your steps toward the trailhead.
- **5.2** Arrive back at the trailhead.

11 Amphitheater Loop Trail

This primitive trail makes a wide loop through rocky hills and valleys in the Richardson Amphitheater east of Moab.

Distance: 3-mile loop
Approximate hiking time: 2 hours
Difficulty: Moderate; 250-foot elevation gain
Trail surface: Single-track dirt trail
Best season: Year-round. Summers are hot.
Other trail users: Mountain bikers

Canine compatibility: Dogs allowed
Fees and permits: No fee or permit
Maps: USGS Dewey
Trail contacts: Bureau of Land Management (BLM), Moab Field Office, 82 E. Dogwood, Moab 84532; (435) 259-2100; www .blm.gov/ut/st/en/fo/moab.html

Finding the trailhead: From Moab, drive north on US 191 to UT 128/River Road just before the Colorado River Bridge. Go right (east) and drive 22 miles on UT 128 to Hittle Bottom Recreation Site/ Campground. Turn left (north) into the campground and park in the parking area on the left past a cattle guard. The trailhead is at the south side of the parking lot. GPS: N 38 45.561' / W 109 19.470'

The Hike

The 3-mile Amphitheater Loop Trail makes an open loop through the wide Richardson Amphitheater south of the Colorado River. This great hike offers a wilderness experience close to UT 128 but is not recommended for beginning hikers. The trail can be hard to follow at times, particularly after rain storms, which may wash away parts of the trail and the cairns which mark it. The trail is, however, close to the

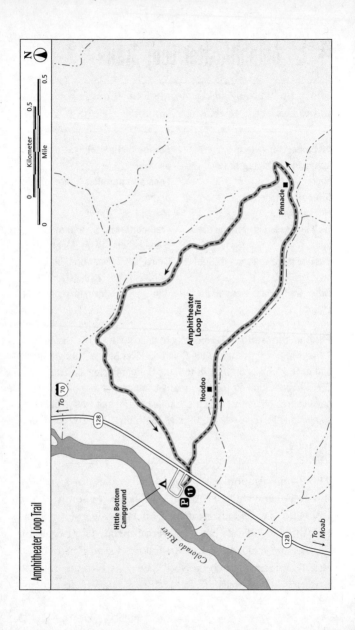

highway and crosses open land with broad views, making it difficult to get lost.

The trail starts at Hittle Bottom Campground, which offers a dozen campsites, a historic homestead, and a put-in and take-out spot for Colorado River rafters. Hittle Bottom is named for Frank Hittle, who left fertile Iowa to homestead this river bottom land in the 1920s.

Start the hike on the south end of the parking area at a BLM sign and trail register. Hike south to a cattle gate right of a cattle guard. Cross the highway and pick up the trail on its south side. The trail bends sharply left and follows the road for 100 feet before turning southeast. After another 100 feet is a Y-shaped trail junction. Take the right fork.

Follow the trail, passing under power lines, for 0.4 mile to the base of some low hills and a strangely shaped hoodoo or rock pinnacle. A viewpoint on the back side of the hoodoo looks north to the Colorado River canyon. If you don't want to do the entire hike, this is a good turn-around point for a 0.8-mile hike.

The trail continues east up the left side of a broad stony wash for 0.9 mile until you're almost to the base of the talus and cliff escarpment forming the east wall of the Richardson Amphitheater. Keep on track by following cairns or rock piles that are strategically placed along the way. Much of this part of the trail was washed out in a massive flash flood in the summer of 2010. Keep to the main wash and you'll be on track.

The trail and wash passes a broken sandstone cliff on the left and reaches a small pinnacle with a large flat balanced rock on its summit to the left. Just past the pinnacle, after 1.3 miles of hiking, the trail reaches a side canyon to the left. The main canyon bends right. Go left and climb the boulder-strewn canyon until the trail exits left and traverses a slope onto a rounded ridge.

Hike northwest along the edge of a canyon until the trail meets up with an old road. Continue northeast, following cairns, as the trail slowly descends. You'll pass a couple junctions marked with posts that indicate the North Alternative and the South Alternative trails. Go left on the South Alternative and descend the old road to some slickrock. Drop left into a wide valley and continue northwest to another signpost. Keep left on the South Alternative trail.

The trail follows the broad wash around the north end of the hills and after 2.2 miles reaches the north end of the trail. Head southwest here, skirting the west edge of the hills and then crossing a wide flat plain to the power lines. The trail continues southwest beneath the lines, before returning back to the trail junction near UT 128. Walk across the highway to the trailhead.

Miles and Directions

- **0.0** Begin at the trailhead at Hittle Bottom.
- **0.1** Arrive at a trail junction. Go right.
- **0.4** Reach a hoodoo and viewpoint.
- **1.3** Turn left and begin traveling up a side canyon.
- **2.2** Reach the north end of hills; follow the trail as it bends left (south).
- **3.0** Return to the trailhead.

12 Mill Canyon Dinosaur Trail

Discover dinosaur bones and petrified wood on this short interpretive hike in Morrison Formation sandstone above a shallow valley northwest of Moab.

Distance: 0.4-mile loop
Approximate hiking time: 30 minutes
Difficulty: Easy; 100-foot elevation gain
Trail surface: Single-track dirt path
Best season: Year-round
Other trail users: None

Canine compatibility: Dogs allowed
Fees and permits: No fee
Maps: USGS Merrimac Butte, *Moab Trails Illustrated Explorer*
Trail contacts: Bureau of Land Management (BLM), Moab Field Office, 82 E. Dogwood, Moab 84532; (435) 259-2100; www .blm.gov/ut/st/en/fo/moab.html

Finding the trailhead: From Moab, drive northwest on US 191 for about 15 miles to a left (west) turn onto a dirt road marked Mill Canyon. The turn is just past highway mile marker 141 (GPS: N 38 43.628' / W 109 43.341'). Bump across railroad tracks and drive 0.6 mile to a junction. Go left here and drive 0.5 mile to a Y-junction. Turn right at the sign for Mill Canyon Dino Trail and drive 0.6 mile up a wash to a parking area and the trailhead. GPS: N 38 42.738' / W 109 44.383'

The Hike

The Mill Canyon Dinosaur Trail is like walking through a natural history museum, except all the exhibits are outside. No panes of glass or partitions separate you from experiencing this wonderful outdoor display of dinosaur bones and petrified wood. This unique trail, which offers a look at a lost world filled with extinct creatures, is a hit with anyone who loves dinosaurs. Its short length makes it especially attractive to dinosaur lovers who happen to be kids.

The 0.4-mile loop trail starts at a parking area above Mill Creek amid low scrubby hills north of Mill Canyon's deep cliff-lined gorge. A couple of BLM interpretive signs introduce you to Mill Canyon's dinosaurs and the ancient environment where they once lived.

The trail explores the Morrison Formation, a widespread rock formation composed of mudstone, siltstone, and sandstone deposited 150 million years ago during the Jurassic Period on broad low-lying plains laced by meandering rivers and covered with dense forests, lakes, and swamps. In contrast with today's arid ecosystem, a warm and moist climate provided abundant plant life, including cycads, ginkgoes, and conifers and a lush understory of ferns and nonflowering plants, which in turn provided forage for massive dinosaurs like Stegosaurus, Camptosaurus, and Camarasaurus. Predators like the fierce Allosaurus also roamed the landscape. Fossilized bones from all of these giants are found along the trail.

These dinosaurs lived in a riparian zone along a large, sluggish river. After dying, their bones were deposited, probably along a river bend, and covered with sand which preserved them. Over eons of time the bones turned to fossils. Water erosion in more recent times dissected this desert area, finally uncovering the fossil deposit on the dry edge of Mill Canyon.

Begin the hike by dropping into shallow Mill Canyon. Cross the dry, sandy creek bed and follow the trail up and south along a broken band of sandstone cliffs. Fifteen stops with interpretive signs are found along the trail, with each

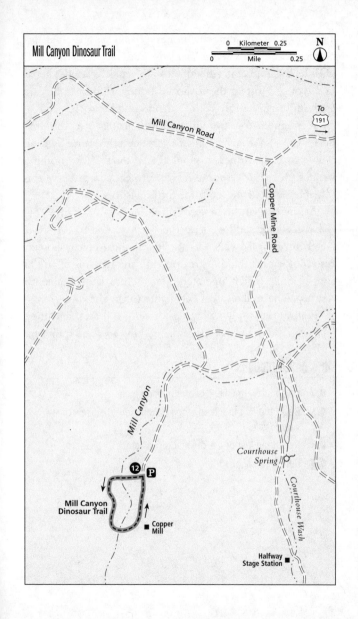

Mill Canyon Dinosaur Trail

0   Kilometer   0.25
0   Mile   0.25

N

Mill Canyon Road

To
191

Copper Mine Road

Mill Canyon

Courthouse
Spring

Courthouse
Wash

12 P

Mill Canyon
Dinosaur Trail

Copper
Mill

Halfway
Stage Station

explaining nearby dinosaur bones. You'll see pieces of leg bones, tail bones, a shoulder blade, and vertebrae from lots of different dinosaurs embedded in the rock as well as petrified wood. Most of the fossilized bones are purple and are easily distinguished from the surrounding bedrock.

Remember to leave all the fossils in place so the next hikers can also enjoy them. If everyone who came by took only a fossil chip then it wouldn't be long before nothing was left. It's your responsibility to protect and preserve this valuable outdoor museum for future visitors.

At the end of the low cliffs, the trail descends into Mill Canyon. Look southwest up the deep canyon to the sheer Determination Towers—Echo Tower and Aeolian Tower. Also look across the dry streambed to the remains of an old copper mill, which operated here in the late nineteenth century. The mill also gave its name to the canyon.

Follow the sandy valley floor north 100 feet, and then follow an old road back up to the parking area and trailhead.

Miles and Directions

0.0 Begin at the trailhead at the parking area.

0.1 Begin the first of fifteen stops pointing out the site's dinosaur fossils.

0.3 Reach the last of the dinosaur-fossil stops.

0.4 Return to trailhead.

13 Copper Ridge Dinosaur Trail

This short uphill hike takes you to one of Utah's best dinosaur trackways.

Distance: 0.3 mile out and back
Approximate hiking time: 30 minutes
Difficulty: Easy; 80-foot elevation gain
Trail surface: Dirt and slickrock surface
Best season: Year-round
Other trail users: None

Canine compatibility: Dogs allowed
Fees and permits: No fee
Maps: USGS Valley City, *Moab Trails Illustrated Explorer*
Trail contacts: Bureau of Land Management (BLM), Moab Field Office, 82 E. Dogwood, Moab 84532; (435) 259-2100; www .blm.gov/ut/st/en/fo/moab.html

Finding the trailhead: From Moab, drive northwest on US 191 for about 23 miles to a right (east) turn onto a dirt road. The turn is 0.75 mile past highway mile marker 148 (GPS: N 38 49.501' / W 109 46.887'). Cross railroad tracks and follow the signed road south and then east around a bluff for 2 miles to a parking area and the trailhead. The road can be muddy and impassable after rain or snow. Don't drive it in bad conditions. GPS: N 38 49.805' / W 109 45.797'

The Hike

The Copper Ridge Dinosaur Trail ascends the slabby western flank of Copper Ridge for 0.15 mile to the Copper Ridge Sauropod Tracksite, one of the most unusual dinosaur sites in the Moab area. The trail, a couple of miles east of US 191, offers a unique glimpse into the distant past when this area was a vast low-lying landscape of broad rivers, swamps, and dense tropical forests. If you hiked the short Dinosaur Tracks Trail at the Poison Spider Mesa trailhead south of Moab along the Colorado River, then you need to drive north to do this short hike to a better trackway.

Dinosaur footprints are uncommon and those that are found are usually uncovered by sheer happenstance. This trackway, found along an old road that climbed to a copper mine on the ridge above, was discovered in 1989. It lies on a stretch of 150-million-year-old sandstone pavement deposited in the Morrison Formation during the Jurassic Period. The widespread Morrison Formation, a thick layer of siltstone, claystone, and sandstone, is well known as the primary dinosaur-bearing rock formation in the American West, with dinosaur bones and skeletons found in Colorado and Utah. Dinosaur tracks are found at about twenty-five Morrison sites.

Start the hike at a BLM sign at the trailhead. Walk west 100 feet to the main trail, an old roadbed, and sign into a register. Hike up the wide trail, lined with large boulders, for 0.15 mile to a broad stretch of slickrock pavement. This is the trackway. A BLM sign on the right gives some details.

Five distinct sets of dinosaur tracks are found on the tilted sandstone pavement. Four of the track sets are from theropods, erect three-toed predators like Allosaurus, while the fifth set is from a large Brontosaurus, possibly a Camarasaurus, Diplodocus, or Apatosaurus. These thirteen Brontosaur prints, the first discovered in Utah, make this site unique. While theropod tracks are relatively common, the huge Brontosaurus tracks are rare.

This Brontosaurus lumbered across a mud plain, probably next to a river channel, leaving deep impressions of his 2-foot-wide hind feet and trace impressions of his smaller

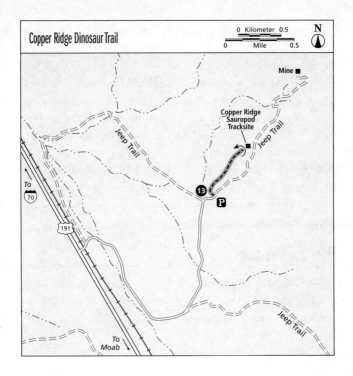

Copper Ridge Dinosaur Trail

0 Kilometer 0.5
0 Mile 0.5

N

Mine ■

Copper Ridge
Sauropod
Tracksite

Jeep Trail

Jeep Trail

13

P

To
70

191

Jeep Trail

To
Moab

forefeet. Another unique aspect of these tracks is that the movement of the giant dinosaur is frozen in stone as he makes a sharp turn to the right, perhaps looking left toward the cry of an Allosaurus. The tracks, appearing as deep round depressions, are on the lower part of the trackway.

Crossing the middle of the Brontosaurus tracks as well as on an upper slab are the large birdlike tracks of various-size theropods like Allosaurus, the most common predator of Morrison times. The tracks, sometimes hard to see here, range in size from 8 to 15 inches long. One of the theropods appears to be limping, alternately taking long and then short steps. The tracks on the higher slab are the largest and best preserved. Look closely and you can see where the sharp claws on each toe plunged into muddy sand as the dinosaur strode across the plain.

After the tracks were made, sand and silt quickly covered them where they were compressed and hardened and then lay underground for millions of years until uplift and erosion unveiled them. This fragile trackway is an outdoor museum and susceptible to human damage. Remember to take only photographs of the footprints. While you may put water in the tracks to make them stand out for photography, do not make plaster casts of them. The plaster damages the porous rock surface and causes long-term damage.

Miles and Directions

0.0 Begin at the trailhead.

0.15 Reach the dinosaur trackway. Retrace your steps to return.

0.3 Arrive back at the trailhead.

14 Lower Courthouse Wash Trail

This primitive hike takes you up a narrow cliff-lined canyon with dense vegetation and pools of water formed by beaver dams.

Distance: 1.8 miles out and back
Approximate hiking time: 1 hour
Difficulty: Moderate; minimal elevation gain
Trail surface: Single-track dirt path
Best season: Year-round
Other trail users: None
Canine compatibility: No dogs allowed
Fees and permits: Daily fee to enter park
Maps: USGS Moab, *Moab Trails Illustrated Explorer*
Trail contacts: Arches National Park, P.O. Box 907, Moab 84532; (435) 719-2299; www .nps.gov/arch/index.htm

Finding the trailhead: From Moab, drive north on US 191. After crossing the Colorado River bridge, drive 0.5 mile and park at a large parking area and the trailhead on the right (north) side of the highway. GPS: N 38 36.417' / W 109 35.226'

The Hike

The Lower Courthouse Wash Trail winds up the floor of a twisting, cliff-lined canyon, offering a good backcountry adventure on the southern edge of Arches National Park. The hike, starting on US 191 rather than in the park, is easily accessible from Moab. Water is usually found in the canyon, especially after summer thunderstorms and during the spring. Beavers have dammed some sections of the canyon, creating great pools of water.

In places, depending on how much flooding has occurred from storms and if the terrain is altered by water, the hike follows different primitive trails. The bottom of the canyon is brushy, with thick stands of willow, tamarisk, and cottonwood trees. Stick to the bottom of the narrow canyon and you'll be fine. If you venture farther up the canyon than the described 0.9-mile hike, be prepared for wading and bushwhacking.

Start the hike at the trailhead sign on the right side of the parking area off US 191. Go right and walk east on a wide paved bike path toward the Colorado River. After 0.2 mile, cross a bridge over Lower Courthouse Wash. On the east side of the bridge, find a trail that heads north into the wash.

The Courthouse Wash rock art site is easily visited from this side of the bridge. It's worth visiting either before or after doing the hike. To find the rock art panel, look up at the cliffs from the end of the bridge—the panel is up there. Follow a small trail uphill to the prehistoric site. The panel, 19 feet high and 52 feet long, has many petroglyphs and pictographs, including large painted ghostlike figures that are probably 2,000 years old. The site was damaged by vandals in 1980.

Hike past a park sign and continue to a fence that marks the boundary of Arches National Park at a grove of cottonwoods. Go past a metal gate to a sign that details the hike up Lower Courthouse Wash. The trail bends right here. Follow the creek bank until short cliffs force you to cross the creek. Hike up a narrow trail on the left bank until you're again forced to cross to the opposite bank.

Continue hiking up the canyon, which bends to the west, leaving the sounds of the highway behind. Tall cliffs line the rim of the canyon. After 0.9 mile you reach a bench

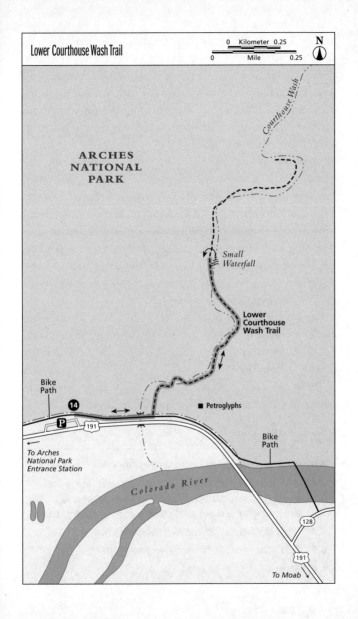

Lower Courthouse Wash Trail

0   Kilometer   0.25

0   Mile   0.25

N

**ARCHES
NATIONAL
PARK**

Courthouse Wash

*Small
Waterfall*

**Lower
Courthouse
Wash Trail**

Bike
Path

14

P 191

■ Petroglyphs

Bike
Path

*To Arches
National Park
Entrance Station*

Colorado River

128

191

To Moab

of pale Kayenta sandstone. The creek tumbles over the polished sandstone and drops 5 feet into a large pool of brown water. Upstream are more pools of still water reflecting cliff and cloud. This small waterfall is the turn-around point for this easy day hike. It's a good place to take off your shoes and dabble your feet in the warm water or to simply sit and soak in the peace and quiet.

Option: If you want to hike farther, continue up the broad canyon above here for another 0.6 mile. The trail, keeping to the west side of the canyon, is easy to follow although it may be covered in spots with brush and branches from recent flash floods. When the canyon begins to narrow, the trail climbs onto a high slope above deep pools formed by beaver dams. Eventually the good trail ends on a cliff above the creek. This point, 1.5 miles from the trailhead, is the best place to turnaround.

If you continue north from here you'll have to wade the creek many times and do some bushwhacking. The Courthouse Wash parking area on the park road is about 5 miles northeast from here.

After returning to the waterfall, hike back down the canyon to the highway bridge and the trailhead.

Miles and Directions

- **0.0** Begin at the trailhead on the north (right) side of US 191.
- **0.2** Hike east on a paved path. Turn north on east side of the bridge. This is a good view spot for the rock art site, to which you may want to make a side hike, now or on the way back.
- **0.3** Cross the Arches National Park boundary fence.
- **0.9** Reach the waterfall. This is the turnaround point.
- **1.8** Arrive back at the trailhead.

15 Park Avenue Trail

Located in the southern sector of Arches National Park, this excellent mile-long hike explores Park Avenue, a sandstone skyscraper–lined canyon.

Distance: 2 miles out and back or 1 mile one way with shuttle pickup

Approximate hiking time: 1 to 1½ hours

Difficulty: Moderate; 250-foot elevation gain

Trail surface: Single-track dirt and slickrock trail. Initial section is wheelchair-accessible.

Best season: Year-round. Summers are hot.

Other trail users: None

Canine compatibility: No dogs allowed

Fees and permits: Daily fee to enter the park

Maps: USGS Arches National Park, *Moab Trails Illustrated Explorer*

Trail contacts: Arches National Park, P.O. Box 907, Moab 84532; (435) 719-2299; www .nps.gov/arch/index.htm

Finding the trailhead: From the Arches National Park entrance station, drive up the park road for 2.5 miles to the Park Avenue trailhead and parking area on the left or north side of the road. GPS: N 38 38.233' / W 109 36.014'. Alternatively, park 3.7 miles from the entrance station at the Courthouse Towers parking area. If one of your party shuttles your vehicle to the north trailhead, meet them at the Courthouse Towers parking. GPS: N 38 37.6866' / W 109 35.974'

The Hike

The 1-mile-long Park Avenue Trail descends down Park Avenue, a spectacular canyon that drains north from the road to Courthouse Wash and the Courthouse Towers sector of Arches National Park. It's best to hike the trail from south to north because it's all downhill that way. If you prefer this easy route, have a driver in your party shuttle your vehicle to the Courthouse Towers parking area at the trail's northern trailhead. Otherwise hike back south up Park Avenue to the southern trailhead for a 2-mile-long hike. Remember, however, that coming back is mostly uphill.

The moderate Park Avenue Trail is easy to follow, with cairns marking the tricky sections. The southern half of the trail is single-track dirt and sand. The northern half follows slickrock pavement along the bed of the dry wash. It's hot in summer, so carry plenty of liquid.

Begin from the southern trailhead on the north side of the park road. Follow a concrete pathway for about 300 feet to an overlook. This initial section is wheelchair accessible. The view from the overlook is spectacular. Imagine the skyscrapers lining Park Avenue, New York City's most famous street, then imagine if those buildings turned to stone—that's Park Avenue, Arches National Park style.

Most tourists turn around at the overlook and trudge the pavement back to their cars, but being an intrepid day hiker, you plunge forward and descend 110 stone steps into upper Park Avenue Canyon. Follow the sandy trail north, slowly descending along benches west of the wash. Strange formations composed of the Entrada Sandstone's Slickrock Member tower above the trail. High on the western rim is Queen Nefertiti, a balanced rock shaped like her Egyptian head, and an obvious thin pillar dubbed Sausage Rock. The Candelebra's vertical face forms the eastern canyon wall.

About 0.5 mile down the canyon, the trail steps into the bottom of the wash. Follow undulating slickrock slabs along

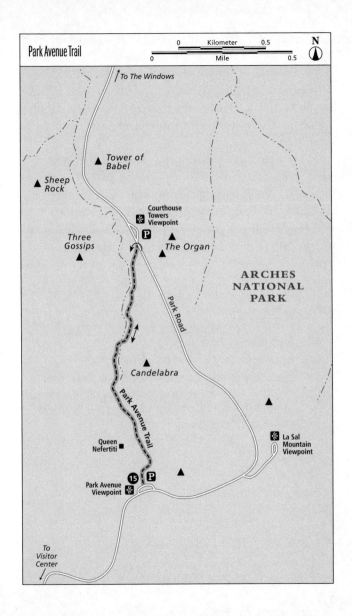

Park Avenue Trail

N

| 0 | Kilometer | 0.5 |
| 0 | Mile | 0.5 |

To The Windows

Tower of Babel

Sheep Rock

Three Gossips

Courthouse Towers Viewpoint

P

The Organ

ARCHES NATIONAL PARK

Park Road

Candelabra

Park Avenue Trail

Queen Nefertiti

La Sal Mountain Viewpoint

15

P

Park Avenue Viewpoint

To Visitor Center

the broad floor of the canyon. Farther along note the sharp spire of Argon Tower on the west side of the canyon. In 1963, the great American climber Layton Kor and a couple friends were the first climbers to reach its small rounded summit. As you trek north, look at The Three Gossips, an obvious formation with three blocky summits, to the northwest.

When the wash bends sharply west, the trail exits right and climbs out of the wash to the park road. The Courthouse Towers parking area is to your left. Cross the road, and hike 100 feet to the parking area. If you don't have someone waiting to pick you up, take a rest and hike south up the trail to the southern trailhead. While it's uphill, the trail is only a mile and the views are just as great the second time.

Miles and Directions

0.0 Begin at the trailhead.

0.05 Reach the end of the paved trail. Descend the hill.

1.0 Reach the park road. Cross to the Courthouse Tower parking area. (This is the recommended pickup location for shuttle hikers.) Turn around and retrace your steps to the trailhead.

2.0 Arrive back at the trailhead.

16 Balanced Rock Trail

This short hike encircles Balanced Rock, one of Arches Park's most precarious rock features. Its first section accommodates wheelchair users.

Distance: 0.3-mile loop
Approximate hiking time: 15 to 30 minutes
Difficulty: Easy; 75-foot elevation gain
Trail surface: Double-track paved and dirt path. First section is wheelchair accessible.
Best season: Year-round
Other trail users: None

Canine compatibility: No dogs allowed
Fees and permits: Daily fee to enter the park
Maps: USGS The Windows Section, *Moab Trails Illustrated Explorer*
Trail contacts: Arches National Park, P.O. Box 907, Moab 84532; (435) 719-2299; www .nps.gov/arch/index.htm

Finding the trailhead: From the Arches visitor center and US 191, drive 9.7 miles on the park road to a right or east turn into the signed Balanced Rock parking area. The trailhead is on the northeast side of the lot. GPS: N 38 42.105' / W 109 33.959'

The Hike

The easy 0.3-mile Balanced Rock Trail encircles Balanced Rock just off the park road west of The Windows section of Arches National Park. The concrete first section of the trail is wheelchair accessible. The rest of the trail is a double-track dirt and slickrock path that is lined with boulders.

Start the hike at the trailhead on the northeast side of the parking area. The wide concrete trail heads east toward

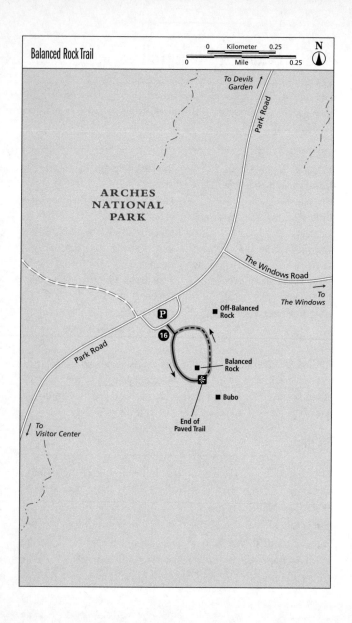

Balanced Rock. Reach a trail junction after 100 yards. The return trail is to the left. Go right on the concrete trail and pass beneath the south side of Balanced Rock. After 0.1 mile the trail reaches a viewpoint at the end of the concrete. This is the turnaround point for wheelchairs.

Balanced Rock, one of Arches National Park's most precarious and fragile natural features, rises to the north. The 128-foot-high spire is composed of two members of Entrada Sandstone. The upper erosion-resistant boulder, weighing 3,500 tons, is shaped from the Slickrock Member, the main arch-forming formation in the park. The twisted lower layer is the Dewey Bridge Member, a soft mudstone that easily erodes. Eventually the soft bottom layer will erode enough to topple the 55-foot balanced boulder.

Go left up a hill from the paved path to a low saddle between Balanced Rock and Bubo, a blocky formation on the right. The trail heads north below Balanced Rock before bending left and descending stone steps to a stretch of slickrock pavement. At the junction with the paved path, go right back to the trailhead.

Miles and Directions

- **0.0** Begin at the trailhead.
- **0.03** Reach the junction. Keep right on paved trail.
- **0.1** Reach the end of the paved trail. Go left on a dirt trail and climb to the east side of Balanced Rock. Then continue toward the trailhead.
- **0.3** Arrive back at the trailhead.

17 The Windows Trail

This popular, easy hike takes you to three of the biggest arches in Arches National Park.

Distance: 0.75 mile lollipop loop
Approximate hiking time: 30 to 45 minutes
Difficulty: Easy; 115-foot elevation gain
Trail surface: Double-track dirt path
Best season: Year-round
Other trail users: None
Canine compatibility: No dogs allowed

Fees and permits: Daily fee to enter the park
Maps: USGS The Windows Section, *Moab Trails Illustrated Explorer*
Trail contacts: Arches National Park, P.O. Box 907, Moab 84532; (435) 719-2299; www .nps.gov/arch/index.htm

Finding the trailhead: From US 191 and the Arches visitor center, drive 9.3 miles north on the park road and turn east (right) to The Windows Road. Drive east for 2.4 miles to the Windows parking area on the east side of the loop at the road's end. GPS: N 38 41.228' / W 109 32.198'

The Hike

The Windows Trail, one of the most popular walks at Arches National Park, makes a 0.75-mile loop hike past three of the park's most spectacular arches. The surface of the wide trail is mostly compacted dirt with stone steps. Come early or stay late to avoid crowds on the trail and to ensure you find a parking spot.

The trailhead is on the east side of the parking area at the end of The Windows Road. A couple of interpretative signs explain how arches form and give information about the trail. Follow the trail east for 0.15 mile to a Y-junction. Take the left trail toward North Window.

Climb a long series of wide stone steps for 0.1 mile to North Window, a wide opening in a fin. Scramble up slickrock to the arch for a great view eastward toward the Colorado River Canyon. From North Window, hike south down stone steps for 0.1 mile to a junction and trail sign. Go left toward South Window on the marked trail. Walk 0.05 mile to a flat viewpoint. South Window is directly north.

The mile-long primitive loop trail begins here. It explores the area behind The Windows before returning to the parking area. Unless you want to do that hike, return back to the trail junction and go left toward Turret Arch. Hike 0.1 mile to a good viewpoint of the arch next to a rock outcrop. Turret Arch has a large keyhole-shaped opening and a smaller window. If you want an up-close view, follow a short trail and scramble up to the arch base.

To finish the hike, descend steps from the Turret Arch viewpoint and hike 0.1 mile back to the first trail junction. Follow the main trail 0.15 mile back to the parking area and trailhead.

Option: For a great optional hike, walk the Windows Primitive Loop. This trail, beginning at the South Window viewpoint at 0.4 mile, makes an open loop around The Windows, passing below them on the east before swinging around the north end of a rock butte and heading back to the parking area. The trail offers solitude and views across the remote Arches backcountry. Note that some uneven

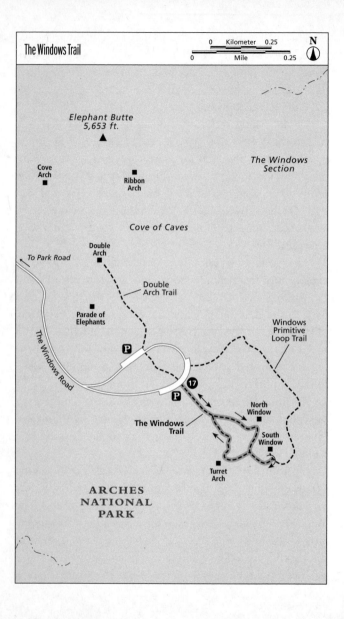

The Windows Trail

0   Kilometer   0.25

0   Mile   0.25

N

Elephant Butte
5,653 ft.

Cove
Arch

Ribbon
Arch

The Windows
Section

Cove of Caves

To Park Road

Double
Arch

Double
Arch Trail

Parade of
Elephants

The Windows Road

P

17

P

Windows
Primitive
Loop Trail

The Windows Trail

North
Window

South
Window

Turret
Arch

ARCHES
NATIONAL
PARK

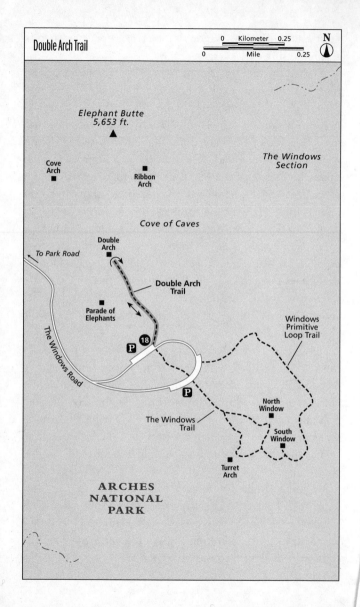

Double Arch Trail

Kilometer 0.25
Mile 0.25

N

Elephant Butte
5,653 ft.

Cove
Arch

Ribbon
Arch

The Windows
Section

Cove of Caves

Double
Arch

To Park Road

Double Arch
Trail

Parade of
Elephants

The Windows Road

P 18

P

Windows
Primitive
Loop Trail

The Windows
Trail

North
Window

South
Window

Turret
Arch

ARCHES
NATIONAL
PARK

terrain makes the primitive loop more challenging than The Windows Trail.

Miles and Directions

0.0 Begin at the trailhead.

0.15 Reach a Y junction. Go left toward the North Window.

0.25 Arrive at the North Window; begin hiking south down stone steps.

0.35 Arrive at a junction. Go left.

0.4 Reach the South Window, where another loop trail begins. Retrace your steps from the South Window to return to the trail junction.

0.45 Arrive at the trail junction. Go left toward Turret Arch.

0.5 Reach Turret Arch.

0.6 Arrive back at the first junction.

0.75 Arrive back at the trailhead.

18 Double Arch Trail

The hike to Double Arch is short and easy. Tucked into a sweeping sandstone amphitheater, this arch is one of the most unusual in Arches National Park.

Distance: 0.6 mile out and back
Approximate hiking time: 15 to 30 minutes
Difficulty: Easy; minimal elevation gain
Trail surface: Single-track dirt path
Best season: Year-round
Other trail users: None
Canine compatibility: No dogs allowed

Fees and permits: Daily fee to enter the park
Maps: USGS The Windows Section, *Moab Trails Illustrated Explorer*
Trail contacts: Arches National Park, P.O. Box 907, Moab 84532; (435) 719-2299; www .nps.gov/arch/index.htm

Finding the trailhead: From US 191 and the Arches visitor center, drive 9.3 miles north on the park road and turn east (right) to The Windows Road. Drive east for 2.4 miles to the Windows parking area on the east side of the loop at the road's end. Continue on the park road for 0.2 mile past the Windows parking to the Double Arch parking area and trailhead on the northwest part of the loop. The trailhead is at the right side of the roadside parking area. GPS: N 38 41.298' / W 109 32.303'. Alternatively, park at the Windows parking area and follow a short trail northwest to the Double Arch trailhead.

The Hike

The Double Arch Trail is an easy hike on a sandy trail to twin arches that span a wide amphitheater. Combine this short hike with The Windows Trail for a spectacular look at some of the park's largest arches.

Start at the trailhead on the right side of the parking area. Interpretative signs explain how Double Arch formed and detail the trail. The wide dirt trail heads northwest, descending into a sandy wash. Double Arch is directly ahead on the south side of Elephant Butte, the 5,653-foot high point of Arches National Park. On your left is a long narrow fin called the Parade of the Elephants, punctuated with a series of arches which resemble a fanciful pack of pachyderms hiking single file with their trunks entwined in their tails.

Continue straight on the sandy trail, which gently rises to sandstone slabs below Double Arch. A good stopping point is the slab directly below the highest span. Double Arch is composed of two long spans. The arch directly above you is the third longest arch in the park at 144 feet and the highest, rising 112 feet. The rear arch is 67 feet wide and 86 feet high.

Double Arch formed from a pothole arch. A pothole in the cliff above filled with water from storms which slowly seeped downward, creating a deep alcove like those on the cliff face to the right of Double Arch. Eventually the pothole dissolved all the sandstone below, leaving the gaping window between the arches. Check out the interpretative sign at the start of the trail for detailed sketches of Double Arch's formation.

If you feel like a mountain goat, scramble up the low-angle slabs below Double Arch to an overlook in the west window with a great view west toward Ham Rock and Balanced Rock. After admiring and photographing the arches, follow the trail back to the parking area.

Miles and Directions

0.0 Begin at the trailhead.

0.3 Arrive at the Double Arch. Turn around and retrace your steps toward the trailhead.

0.6 Arrive back at the trailhead.

19 Delicate Arch Trail

This excellent hike takes you up a steep trail to Delicate Arch, Moab's most famous arch.

Distance: 3 miles out and back
Approximate hiking time: 2 hours
Difficulty: More challenging; 530-foot elevation gain
Trail surface: Double-track dirt and slickrock trail
Best season: Year-round
Other trail users: None

Canine compatibility: No dogs allowed
Fees and permits: Daily fee to enter the park
Maps: USGS The Windows Section and Big Bend
Trail contacts: Arches National Park, P.O. Box 907, Moab 84532; (435) 719-2299; www.nps.gov/arch/index.htm

Finding the trailhead: From US 191 and the Arches visitor center, drive 11.8 miles north on the park road and turn east (right) on a signed road to Delicate Arch. Drive east for 1.2 miles to the Delicate Arch Trail parking area on the north (left) side of the road. GPS: N 38 44.140' / W 109 31.231'

The Hike

This excellent 1.5-mile trail, one of Moab's best hikes, ends at Delicate Arch, an iconic Utah landmark that symbolizes the red-rock canyon country. You may have seen it on postage stamps or Utah license plates, but nothing is like seeing it up close and in person.

This popular trail is easy to follow, with some sections marked with cairns, and is moderate in difficulty. The uphill trail gains 530 feet, mostly up a sloping slickrock slab with a gradual grade. Steep drop-offs are found at the end of the trail and near the arch. Watch your footing if the rock surface is wet or icy. The trail is challenging for many hikers; don't underestimate the trail and how long it will take to hike it. Little shade is found along the trail so it is usually hot in summer. Bring water, use sunscreen, and wear a hat.

Because the trail is one of the busiest in Arches National Park, plan to share the trail and the viewpoints with other hikers. A sign at the trailhead reminds you: DON'T BE AN ARCH HOG! Hikers travel from all over the world to see and photograph Delicate Arch. They are often frustrated by inconsiderate folks who insist on parking themselves under the arch and not moving for an hour. It's best to sit on the slabs opposite the arch to enjoy the view and let the photographers make their images without people in the arch. This is especially true in late afternoon and sunset when the best light floods across Delicate Arch.

Begin your Delicate Arch hike at the trailhead on the east side of the parking area. A couple of signs explain the trail and offer safety tips. There are also toilets, recycle bins, and trash cans. No water is available, so make sure you fill your bottles at the park visitor center beforehand.

Walk east on the broad dirt trail to the historic Wolfe Ranch. Pioneer rancher and Civil War veteran John Wesley Wolfe emigrated here from Ohio and settled on 100 acres along Salt Creek. For a decade his family lived here in a one-room cabin with a corral. The present log cabin was built in 1906. Four years later he moved back to Ohio and died in 1913 at the age of 84. A short spur trail encircles the cabin. Don't touch or enter the cabin and the corrals.

After returning to the main trail, go left and cross a bridge over Salt Creek, one of the major drainages in Arches National Park. On the far side of the bridge, another spur

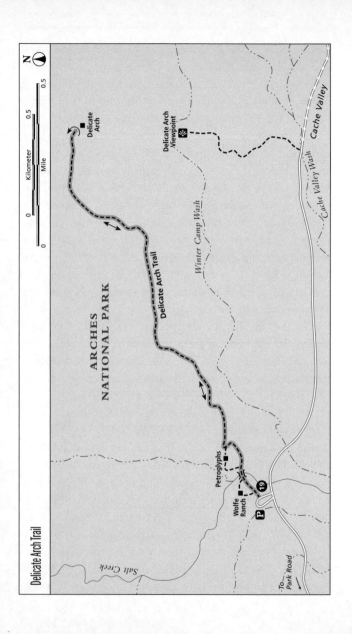

loop trail goes left for 0.1 mile to a beautiful panel of Ute Indian petroglyphs pecked into the dark varnish on a short cliff band. Visit them now and then return to the main trail on the outer loop or on your return hike.

The next trail segment climbs across low shale hills and angles up a dry wash. After 0.7 mile you reach the base of a long tawny sandstone slab. Climbing this sloping 0.3-mile slab is the crux of the trail for most hikers. It's best to wear grippy rubber-soled shoes rather than leather ones. Hike up the slab, following cairns that mark the easiest path upward. Angle left at the top and cross a rock rib after a mile of hiking.

Continue northeast on the dirt and slickrock trail up a shallow valley to a wide sandstone amphitheater. Angle right and hike along a stone pavement trail below a cliff. The last trail segment edges across a sloping rock slab to the final overlook. This section is exposed, with a steep cliff below. Keep children under control. The 4-foot-wide trail, chiseled out of the cliff face, gently ascends above a shallow canyon to the left. Look closely at the cliff on the opposite side of the canyon and locate a pothole arch at its top. Farther along is small Frame Arch to your right. It got its name because it frames Delicate Arch perfectly. Stop at it on your way back for photographs so you don't spoil the final surprise view on the trail.

The hike finishes on a rounded slickrock ridge opposite Delicate Arch and above a sweeping arena of smooth Entrada Sandstone. The 56-foot-high freestanding arch, the final eroded remnant of a fin, rises above a ridge. The view is simply beautiful, especially in the late afternoon when warm sunlight glows on the arch. Beyond rise the snow-capped La Sal Mountains.

Early cowboys called the arch The Chaps and The Schoolmarm's Bloomers until Frank Beckwith dubbed it Delicate Arch in 1933 during the Arches National Monument Scientific Expedition. Delicate Arch is a very fragile mature arch. Like its famous brother Landscape Arch, it could fall at any time. Note the horizontal thinning on the left leg and the obvious deep crack that splits the summit block. We're lucky to see this elderly marvel of erosion before its eventual topple.

Enjoy the view from rounded boulders at the viewpoint. If you're sure-footed you can scramble over to the arch base. Just remember not to be an arch hog. Let the photographers get their images without you in them!

After soaking in the magical ambience of Delicate Arch and its sandstone surroundings, follow the trail back 1.5 miles to the trailhead and parking. It goes fast since the trail is all downhill.

Miles and Directions

0.0   Begin at the trailhead.

0.7   Reach the base of a sandstone slab and scramble up.

1.0   Arrive at the top of the slab, where the trail bends north.

1.5   Reach the Delicate Arch viewpoint. Turn around and retrace your steps toward the trailhead.

3.0   Arrive back at the trailhead.

20 Broken Arch and Sand Dune Arch Trails

This easy scenic hike reaches a couple of unique arches in the southern sector of Devil's Garden, an area well known for its eroded rock fins and canyons.

Distance: 1.7 miles out and back

Approximate hiking time: 1 hour

Difficulty: Easy; 50-foot elevation loss and gain

Trail surface: Single- and double-track dirt and sand path

Best season: Year-round

Other trail users: None

Canine compatibility: No dogs allowed

Fees and permits: Daily fee to enter the park

Maps: USGS Mollie Hogans, *Moab Trails Illustrated Explorer*

Trail contacts: Arches National Park, P.O. Box 907, Moab 84532; (435) 719-2299; www .nps.gov/arch/index.htm

Finding the trailhead: From US 191 and the park visitor center, drive north on the park road for 16 miles to a large parking area for the Sand Dune Arch and Broken Arch trails on the right (east) side of the road. The trailhead is on the east side of the lot. GPS: N 38 52.313' / W 109 42.257'

The Hike

This hike combines the 0.15-mile Sand Dune Arch and 0.65-mile Broken Arch Trails into a 1.7-mile scenic hike among sandstone fins and across a southern part of Devil's Garden. For a longer hike you can add a 0.7-mile loop from Broken Arch to the park campground then back to Broken Arch Trail.

Both trails are easy to follow and have either a dirt or sand surface. The short Sand Dune Arch Trail is especially popular with kids, who enjoy playing in the sand below the arch.

Start the hike at the trailhead on the east side of the parking area. The trail heads east on a wide path just north of some high sandstone fins. After 0.1 mile you reach a signed trail junction. Go right toward Sand Dune Arch.

Hike south, squeezing through a narrow gap between the towering fins and enter a sandy canyon walled with soaring sandstone cliffs. Walk past a small blocky pinnacle on either its right or left side. After hiking 0.1 mile from the junction, you reach Sand Dune Arch.

Sand Dune Arch, a park favorite, is a small span tucked between fins. A sand dune, usually well tracked with footprints, sprawls below the arch into the narrow canyon below. Kids love to romp across the sand. It's also a good arch to visit on warm days since there is plentiful shade in the canyon. Do not, however, climb on top of the arch, which is against park policy, or jump off the arch into the sand.

After enjoying this intimate arch, hike back north 0.1 mile to the trail junction and go right. Follow the single-track sandy trail northeast toward Broken Arch, visible on the right side of the rock fins ahead of you. The trail crosses a wide plain covered with sagebrush, saltbush, and Mormon tea and after 0.4 mile (0.5 mile from the trailhead) reaches a signed three-way junction. Continue straight to Broken Arch. A left turn here makes a 0.7-mile loop to the campground before cutting south to Broken Arch.

Go straight on the trail as it skirts the southern edge of a series of vertical fins and then follows a dry wash to Broken

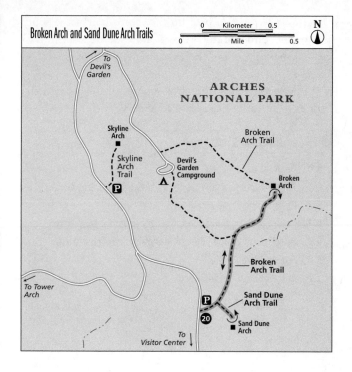

Arch, reaching it 0.7 mile from the trailhead. Broken Arch, while less than a mile from the park road, offers a back-country experience. Lots of hikers go to Sand Dune Arch, while fewer trek back to Broken Arch. Those who do find solitude, quiet, and lots of great scenic views. Scramble up and sit in the shade of the arch on a hot day. You'll get long views to the southwest to the La Sal Mountains.

Option: If you want to add an additional 0.7-mile loop to your hike, clamber through Broken Arch and pick up the trail on the other side. Follow the single-track trail northwest to Devil's Garden Campground; go left on the campground road and pick up the return trail at the south end of the campground loop. Follow that trail southeast through fins and rejoin the Broken Arch trail at its second junction.

Otherwise, follow the Broken Arch Trail back to the trailhead and parking area by retracing your steps.

Miles and Directions

0.0 Begin at the trailhead.

0.1 Reach a trail junction. Go right toward Sand Dune Arch.

0.2 Reach Sand Dune Arch.

0.3 Return to the trail junction. Go right toward Broken Arch.

0.7 Reach another trail junction. Keep right along the wash.

1.0 Reach Broken Arch.

1.7 Arrive back at the trailhead.

21 Skyline Arch Trail

This short hike leads to the base of Skyline Arch, one of Arches National Park's newest spans.

Distance: 0.4 mile out and back

Approximate hiking time: 15 to 30 minutes

Difficulty: Easy; 50-foot elevation gain

Trail surface: Single-track dirt path

Best season: Year-round

Other trail users: None

Canine compatibility: No dogs allowed

Fees and permits: Daily fee to enter the park

Maps: USGS Arches National Park, *Moab Trails Illustrated Explorer*

Trail contacts: Arches National Park, P.O. Box 907, Moab 84532; (435) 719-2299; www .nps.gov/arch/index.htm

Finding the trailhead: From US 191 and the park visitor center, drive north on the park road to the Skyline Arch parking area and trailhead on the right (east) side of the road about a half mile before the end of the road at Devil's Garden. The trailhead is on the right side of the parking area. GPS: N 38 46.319' / W 109 35.455'

The Hike

This is a great easy hike for beginners, kids, and senior citizens. The 0.4-mile round-trip hike out to Skyline Arch and back is a fun adventure to one of the national park's newest arches.

Start the hike at the trailhead on the right side of a parking area on the east side of the park road before it dead

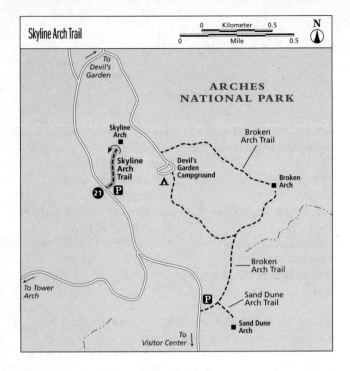

Skyline Arch Trail

| 0 | Kilometer | 0.5 |
| 0 | Mile | 0.5 |

N

ARCHES
NATIONAL PARK

To
Devil's
Garden

Skyline
Arch

Skyline
Arch
Trail

Broken
Arch Trail

Devil's
Garden
Campground

Broken
Arch

21 P

To Tower
Arch

Broken
Arch Trail

Sand Dune
Arch Trail

P

To
Visitor Center

Sand Dune
Arch

ends at Devil's Garden. Skyline Arch is visible north of the trailhead. An interpretative sign details the arch's formation.

Hike north up a dry wash between a couple of lumpy formations, then walk across a sandy area studded with salt-bush and scattered juniper. As you near the arch, the trail swings around the left side of a narrow sandstone fin and enters a quiet canyon.

The trail ends at a jumble of large angular boulders that fell out of the arch one night in 1940. A huge boulder filled half the arch before it fell and splattered where you're standing, forming today's arch, which measures 71 feet long and 33.5 feet high. After admiring Skyline Arch, retrace your footsteps back to the parking area.

Miles and Directions

0.0 Begin at the trailhead.

0.2 Reach the end of the trail below the arch. Retrace your steps to return to the trailhead.

0.4 Arrive back at the trailhead.

22 Devil's Garden Trail

This excellent backcountry hike leads you past pinnacles and through a maze of fins to a hidden arch in the remote Klondike Bluffs sector of Arches National Park.

Distance: 2.35 miles out and back
Approximate hiking time: 1 to 2 hours
Difficulty: Easy to Landscape Arch, more challenging beyond; 250-foot elevation gain
Trail surface: Single-track dirt path
Best season: Year-round
Other trail users: None

Canine compatibility: No dogs allowed
Fees and permits: Daily fee to enter the park
Maps: USGS Mollie Hogans, *Moab Trails Illustrated Explorer*
Trail contacts: Arches National Park, P.O. Box 907, Moab 84532; (435) 719-2299; www .nps.gov/arch/index.htm

Finding the trailhead: From US 191 and the park visitor center, drive north on the park road for 19 miles to a large parking area at the end of the road at Devil's Garden. There are 150 parking spaces; the lot is usually filled by midmorning on busy days. Arrive before 9 a.m. to get a spot. No overflow parking is allowed. The trailhead is on the north side of the lot next to toilets and a trailhead kiosk. GPS: N 38 46.988' / W 109 35.708'

The Hike

The Devil's Garden Trail, along with the Delicate Arch Trail, is simply not to be missed by any Arches hiker. The hike explores a maze of fins that contains the most concentrated collection of arches in the world, including Landscape Arch, considered the world's longest natural arch. This hike takes you to Landscape as well as Pine Tree and Tunnel Arches. If you also do the 2.9-mile primitive loop trail beyond Landscape Arch, you'll see Wall, Partition, Navajo, Double O, and Private Arches as well as several smaller ones if you look carefully.

The trail, beginning at the end of the park road, is very popular. The 150-space parking area quickly fills up at peak times, and there is no overflow parking. Plan to arrive early on weekends or during prime arch-hunting seasons in spring and autumn to do the hike.

The double-track trail is well defined with minimal grades and easy hiking. Remember to bring water, especially in summer, and a hat and sunscreen. Little shade is found along the trail.

Begin the hike at the Devil's Garden trailhead on the north side of the parking area. A couple of signs interpret the trail and the area. There is also a water tap and fountain for filling your water bottles, trash and recycling receptacles, restrooms, a bike rack, and a picnic table. Southeast of the trailhead is the park's 50-site Devil's Garden Campground.

Follow the trail 0.25 mile northwest from the trailhead, passing between two massive fins to an open area and trail junction. A right turn goes east to Pine Tree and Tunnel Arches. Continue straight though, you'll detour to see the arches on your return hike.

Continue hiking northwest on the wide rock-lined trail through shallow sandy valleys between soaring sandstone fins and walls. You reach a trail junction at 0.75 mile in a sandy wash. The primitive trail comes in from the right here. Continue straight on the main trail, threading up a shallow wash toward obvious Landscape Arch. After 0.9 mile, just past the start of the primitive Devil's Garden Trail,

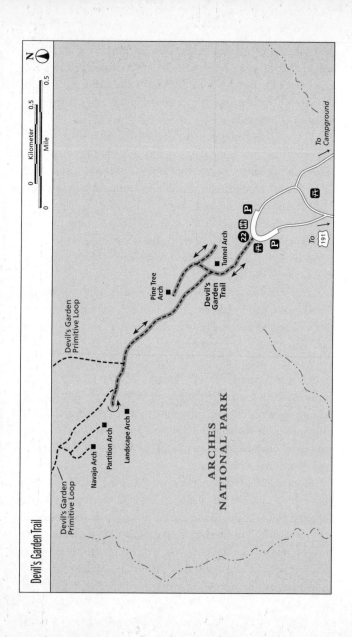

Devil's Garden Trail

you reach the hike's end near the right side of the arch. Don't go outside the fenced area so the fragile cryptobiotic soil isn't damaged by your footsteps. After several rockfalls the arch is also considered very unstable, so the trail under the arch is closed for public safety.

Landscape Arch is a freak of nature, a slender elegant span that appears to defy the laws of gravity and could collapse on any given day. Geologists consider this marvel to be the longest natural stone span in the world with a length, measured in 2004, of 290 feet, slightly longer than 287-foot-long Kolob Arch in Zion National Park, and a thickness of 11 feet. Three large sandstone slabs have fallen from the underside of the arch since 1991, making it thinner and more fragile. The arch is best seen and photographed from the fenced viewpoint at the end of the spur trail with its long span etched against the morning sky.

After admiring the arch, return 0.1 mile to a trail junction. A left turn here would take you on the optional Devil's Garden Primitive Loop, a 2.9-mile trail that explores the northern part of Devil's Garden. The described trail continues to the right. After 0.55 mile you'll reach the trail junction for Pine Tree and Tunnel Arches that you passed earlier. Go left on the wide trail and descend a hill for 0.05 mile to a junction. Go right for 0.1 mile to the viewpoint for Tunnel Arch, a window poking through a thick fin. Return back to the junction and go right. Hike 0.15 mile to Pine Tree Arch, a tall arch that overlooks a maze of fins.

After viewing Pine Tree Arch, return back to the main trail and go left. Hike 0.25 mile back to the parking area and water fountain.

Option: After reaching Landscape Arch and returning to the main trail, a left turn leads to the Devil's Garden

Primitive Loop. This more challenging trail is a single-track path that crosses sand and slickrock and requires rock scrambling in a few spots. If you don't want to do the entire 2.9-mile loop, consider hiking the first 1.2 miles out to Double O Arch. This trail section mostly entails easy hiking on sandstone and passes several arches including Partition and Navajo Arches and the remnants of the now collapsed Wall Arch.

Miles and Directions

0.0   Begin at the trailhead at the end of the park road.

0.25 Reach a junction with a spur trail to Tunnel and Pine Tree Arches.

0.75 Arrive at a junction with primitive loop trail. Stay left.

0.8   Reach another junction with the primitive loop trail.

0.9   Arrive at Landscape Arch, which is the turnaround point. Begin retracing your steps.

1.55 Reach the junction with a spur to Tunnel and Pine Tree Arches. Go left.

1.7   Arrive at Tunnel Arch. Return back to the junction and this time go right.

1.85 Arrive at Pine Tree Arch. Return to junction and turn left to return to main trail.

2.1   Return to the main trail. Go left.

2.35 Return to the trailhead and parking area.

23 Tower Arch Trail

This excellent backcountry hike leads you past pinnacles and through a maze of fins to a hidden arch in the remote Klondike Bluffs sector of Arches National Park.

Distance: 3.4 miles out and back

Approximate hiking time: 2 hours

Difficulty: Moderate; 250-foot elevation gain

Trail surface: Single-track dirt path

Best season: Year-round

Other trail users: None

Canine compatibility: No dogs allowed

Fees and permits: Daily fee to enter the park

Maps: USGS Klondike Bluffs, *Moab Trails Illustrated Explorer*

Trail contacts: Arches National Park, P.O. Box 907, Moab 84532; (435) 719-2299; www .nps.gov/arch/index.htm

Finding the trailhead: From US 191 and the visitor center, follow the park road for 16 miles to a left or west turn onto Salt Valley Road. Follow the gravel road northwest up Salt Valley for 7.1 miles to a marked Y junction. Go left or northwest on the marked Klondike Bluffs Road and drive 1.5 miles until the road dead-ends at the trailhead and a restroom. (Note: Don't take the first left turn, which is just before the Klondike Bluffs Road, since it becomes a rough four-wheel-drive road. Also do not drive on the Salt Valley Road after heavy rain or if the weather appears threatening. It follows a drainage that is prone to flash flooding.) GPS: N 38 47.540' / W 109 40.519'

The Hike

The Tower Arch Trail makes a great half-day hike to a remote arch in Klondike Bluffs, a maze of fins, buttresses, towers, and bluffs in the northwest corner of Arches National

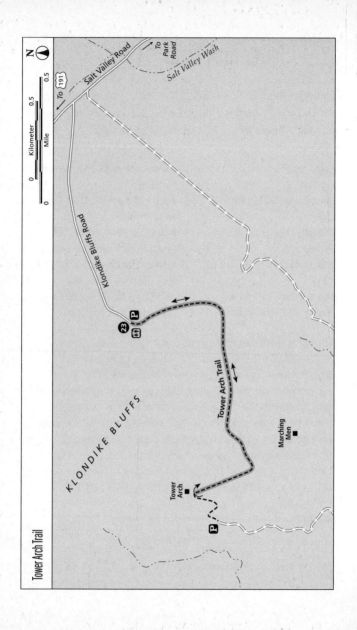

Tower Arch Trail

Park. After you've sampled the park's easier classic hikes like Delicate Arch and Park Avenue, do Tower Arch Trail.

The 1.7-mile, out-and-back trail is mostly easy to follow, with a slickrock section marked by cairns or rock stacks to point the way. The lightly used trail is in a more remote location than other park attractions, so come prepared. Carry lots of water, wear proper shoes and a hat, and use sunscreen.

Begin from the trailhead on the west side of the parking area. A park sign details the trail and offers safety tips and a map. The trail heads southwest, climbing sandstone slabs and boulders to a broad bench. Continue south on the bench to another rise and scramble up more slabs to a higher bench and the ridgeline at 0.4 mile. The trail is well marked on this initial ascent.

Follow the sandy trail west, gently descending a long open slope with wide scenic views. To your right is Klondike Bluffs proper, a stunning escarpment of jutting fins and buttresses split by deep cracks. As you descend west, the trail crosses patches of slickrock pavement or bare bedrock. Keep an eye out for cairns as you hike to keep on the trail.

After a mile of hiking you reach a broad sandy wash that drains south from the bluffs. The Marching Men, a row of slender sandstone pinnacles, perch on a ridge to the south. The trail leaves the wash and climbs a steep slope of loose pink sand to a large narrow fin. Turn north here and pass below the right side of the fin.

The next 0.3-mile trail section tracks across sand dunes anchored with scrubby junipers and threads through narrow canyons between fins. Follow the cairns to keep on course. After crossing a ledge above a sandy slot, the trail dips into a wash. A forming arch is in the cliff face to the right.

As you hike north into the wash, look up right at a free-standing spire shaped like an ice cream cone with a scoop of white rock on top. Tower Arch is directly below the tower. Just before Tower Arch is a trail junction. Continue straight to the arch. A left turn heads west a short distance to a four-wheel-drive parking area and road. At the arch, scramble up slabs on its left side and traverse right into the arch.

Tower Arch, a 92-foot-long by 43-foot-wide opening, is the sixth-largest arch out of 2,200 arches and windows in Arches National Park. On a hot day, stretch out below the arch and enjoy the shade and study its amazing symmetry and fragility. Also note an inscription carved by Hungarian-born prospector Alex Ringhoffer in 1922. Ringhoffer's explorations of the Klondike Bluffs area, which he originally named Devil's Garden, led to the establishment of Arches National Monument in 1929.

Finish the hike by following the trail back to the parking area. Pay attention to the slickrock section past the dry wash since it's easy to get off trail. Watch for the cairns.

Miles and Directions

0.0 Begin at the Klondike Bluffs trailhead.

0.4 Ascend to top of ridge.

1.0 Reach a sandy wash north of Marching Men.

1.3 Ascend to the top of a sand hill.

1.7 Arrive at Tower Arch. Retrace your steps to return to the trailhead.

3.4 Arrive at the trailhead.

24 Dead Horse Point Loop Trail

This easy loop around the airy perimeter of Dead Horse Point offers stunning panoramic views.

Distance: 1.1-mile loop
Approximate hiking time: 30 minutes to 1 hour
Difficulty: Easy; 50-foot elevation gain
Trail surface: Single- and double-track paved, dirt, and slickrock trail. First trail section is wheelchair accessible.
Best season: Year-round. Summers are hot.

Other trail users: None
Canine compatibility: Dogs allowed on leash
Fees and permits: Fee required to enter park
Maps: USGS Musselman Arch, *Moab Trails Illustrated Explorer*
Trail contacts: Dead Horse Point State Park, P.O. Box 609, Moab, UT 84532-0609; (435) 259-2614; www.utah.com/state parks/dead_horse.htm

Finding the trailhead: Drive northwest from Moab on US 191 for 10 miles. Turn left (south) on UT 313 between mile markers 135 and 136. From I-70 to the north, drive 19 miles south to UT 313. Follow UT 313 south for 22 miles to Dead Horse Point State Park. Look for a sharp left (east) turn at a road junction on UT 313 at The Knoll; go left at the sign for Dead Horse Point. GPS: N 38 28.212' / W 109 44.373'

The Hike

This short, easy trail explores the southern rim of Dead Horse Point, a high, narrow peninsula surrounded by vertical sandstone cliffs, and offers some of the most spectacular panoramic viewpoints in the Moab area. The trail lies in 5,362-acre Dead Horse Point State Park, northeast of the

Island in the Sky district of Canyonlands National Park and 12 air miles southwest of Moab. The park is a visitor-friendly destination with 10 miles of hiking trails, mountain bike trails, a twenty-one-site campground, picnic areas, and a visitor center.

The first part of the trail to the main overlook has a pavement surface and is wheelchair accessible. Another 0.3-mile trail section from the main overlook to a viewpoint on the east side of the rim has an asphalt surface and is also wheelchair and stroller accessible. The rest of the trail has either a dirt or rock-pavement surface. The trail on the west side of the park road is primitive and can be difficult to follow in places. Look for cairns or stacks of rocks to mark the way.

The trail begins at the end of the park road. A large parking lot, restrooms, and picnic tables are here. The trailhead, on the southwest corner of the parking area, has an interpretive sign about the Colorado River, Dead Horse Point, and Utah state parks. The concrete trail heads south up a slight hill for 0.05 mile to Dead Horse Point, a stunning viewpoint above the Colorado River, 2,000 feet below, and its sinuous canyon. A large metal ramada offers welcome shade on hot days.

The Dead Horse Point view is simply exceptional. Beyond the Colorado River and its canyon to the southeast stretches the Needles District of Canyonlands National Park and the humped Abajo Mountains, while the La Sal Mountains poke above a maze of sandstone fins called Behind the Rocks to the east. From the first overlook, walk west to a higher viewpoint that looks into Shafer Canyon and then return east and follow a waist-high stone retaining wall along the abrupt cliff edge. Watch children and don't climb over the wall. The cliff drops sheer for 300 feet to talus slopes below.

The wide trail, mostly asphalt with occasional bits of slickrock, follows the eastern edge of the point. Along this section you can stop at benches interspersed along the trail and enjoy a series of stunning viewpoints. A trail junction is reached at 0.35 mile. Go right on a paved spur for 0.05 mile to another great overlook. Below spreads a barren land of cliff and cactus to the La Sal Mountains. Near the river are settling ponds, dyed blue to increase evaporation; these are used for drying potash, which is later dried, bagged, and shipped as a water softener.

Return to the main trail and go right. The paved trail ends here so if you don't want to do the primitive trail section, turn around and retrace your steps back to Dead Horse Point overlook and the parking area.

The trail goes northwest and descends stone steps. Follow it around a rock knob on slickrock marked with cairns to a pullout on the road. Hike up the trail on the right side of the road to a sign on the right and cross the road to its west side at 0.6 mile and go left. Two trails continue north from here for 2 miles along both the eastern and western edges of the island to the park visitor center.

Right here you're on The Neck, the narrowest part of the plateau peninsula. It was here that cowboys created a fence of old logs, such as the one seen on both sides of the road, as a horse corral to keep wild mustangs. After culling out the best horses, the legend goes, the rest of the horses were left and died of thirst, which gave the area its name Dead Horse Point.

The next 0.5-mile segment follow a primitive trail along the rim rock west of the road. The trail dips and rolls,

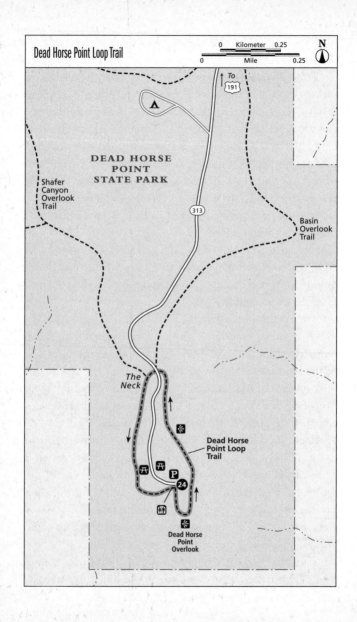

crossing sections of slickrock pavement and a narrow dirt path past scattered junipers and a picnic area. You'll find lots of great views into the Shafer Basin to the west. Sunset Butte is the obvious pointed formation rising directly to the west. Keep on track by following cairns sprinkled along the trail. When you near the tip of the point, the trail intersects a paved trail. Go left on it to the restrooms, parking area, and trailhead.

Miles and Directions

0.0   Begin at the trailhead.

0.05 Reach Dead Horse Point overlook. Go left.

0.35 Arrive at a junction. Go right on a short spur to another overlook and return to the main trail.

0.6   Cross the road at The Neck.

1.1   Arrive back at the trailhead and parking.

25 Aztec Butte Trail

Easy hiking on a sandy trail leads to a scramble up the slick-rock flank of Aztec Dome to several Native American ruins below the flat summit.

Distance: 1.5 miles out and back

Approximate hiking time: 1½ to 2 hours

Difficulty: Moderate; 225-foot elevation gain. Requires scrambling over slickrock.

Trail surface: Single and double-track dirt and slickrock trail

Best season: Year-round

Other trail users: None

Canine compatibility: No dogs allowed

Fees and permits: Daily fee to enter park

Maps: USGS Musselman Arch and Upheaval Dome, *Moab Trails Illustrated Explorer*

Trail contacts: Canyonlands National Park, 2282 SW Resource Blvd., Moab 84532; (435) 719-2313 or (435) 259-4351 for backcountry information; www.nps.gov/cany/index.htm

---

Finding the trailhead: From Moab, drive northwest on US 191 to UT 313. Turn left (south) on UT 313 and follow the paved road south to Canyonlands National Park. From the visitor center, drive southwest 6.5 miles to a road junction. Go right (west) on Upheaval Dome Road; after 0.8 mile turn right (north) into the Aztec Butte parking lot. GPS: N 38 23.610' / W 109 52.916'

The Hike

The mile-long Aztec Butte Trail climbs to the flat summit of 6,312-foot Aztec Butte, one of the highest points on the Island in the Sky in Canyonlands National Park. The trail offers easy hiking on a sandy trail and then scrambles up slickrock slabs to the flat summit. The hike highlights are great views and several ancient granaries used by Ancestral Puebloan people over 1,000 years ago.

The bare slickrock climbing section up the rock pyramid has difficult footing for many hikers. It's advisable to wear a sturdy shoe with a rubber rather than leather sole to achieve maximum friction on the smooth rock surfaces. Follow cairns or small rock piles, marking the easiest route up the butte, to the summit. Remember that you also have to climb down this same route. The route is not advised for anyone afraid of heights. Also keep off the exposed summit during lightning storms.

Start the hike at the trailhead on the east side of the parking area. A park sign details the trail and has a map with granary locations. The trail descends gentle slopes down to a sandy wash below a low rock butte and then follows the wash east, skirting the butte's southern edge. A trail junction is at 0.4 mile. A side trail goes left here and scrambles up an easy slab to the top of the first butte, where you'll find some granaries. Save this detour for your return trip.

Continue straight on the main trail to the base of Aztec Butte's west face, a half mile from the trailhead. Above you towers 200-foot-high Aztec Butte, which resembles Mexico's famed Pyramid of the Sun, a flat-topped pyramid built by the Aztec civilization. Aztec Butte is composed of Navajo Sandstone, a 170-million-year-old sand dune formation deposited during the Jurassic Period during the age of the dinosaurs. As you climb the butte, note the sandstone's cross-bedding, which indicates the petrified dunes and the prevailing winds during their deposition.

The fun part of the hike, 0.25 mile from base to summit, now begins. Scramble up a low-angle sandstone slab and

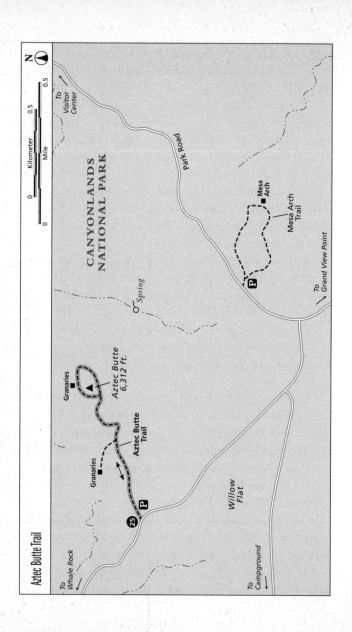

Aztec Butte Trail

N

Kilometer
0   0.5
0   0.5
Mile

To
Visitor
Center

Park Road

CANYONLANDS
NATIONAL PARK

Spring

Mesa
Arch

Mesa Arch
Trail

P

To
Grand View Point

Granaries

Aztec Butte
6,312 ft.

Granaries

Aztec Butte
Trail

P

25

To
Whale Rock

Willow
Flat

To
Campground

then head up right to a group of junipers and piñon pines on a gravel terrace. Go right along the terrace, following cairns, to a final exposed slickrock slab and the broad summit.

Follow the trail across the top of the summit to its east edge and enjoy stunning views north into deep Trail Canyon, which drains northwest to Taylor Canyon and the Green River. On the east side of the summit, look for a trail which descends onto a ledge system. Follow the narrow trail left or northwest below the summit rock cap to several granaries built by the Ancestral Puebloan people.

Granaries were built by the Fremont people, a semi-nomadic group that inhabited central Utah from 700 to 2,000 years ago. Practicing incipient agriculture, they would plant maize and squash in moist areas, returning later to harvest the crops. Granaries, small masonry structures built in sheltered alcoves under cliffs, were used to store vital seeds as well as tools. One of the granaries on Aztec Butte is well preserved. Remember that all archeological sites are protected. Don't climb inside the granaries or remove any artifacts you might find.

After mulling over the lives of the ancient ones, follow the trail left and climb over a boulder to the north side of the summit. Follow the narrow trail back to the edge of the butte's west face and downclimb the slabs to the base.

If you want to view more granaries, take the short trail on the right when you're returning and scramble about 100 feet to the top of the lower butte. A couple of well-preserved granaries are on the north side of the butte.

Then retrace your steps back down and follow the sandy trail back to the trailhead.

Miles and Directions

0.0 Begin at the trailhead.

0.4 Arrive at the junction with the trail to a small butte and granaries. Continue straight on the main trail.

0.5 Reach the base of Aztec Butte and begin climbing.

0.75 Arrive at the summit of Aztec Butte. Then return the way you came.

1.1 Arrive back at the trail junction. Go straight or for an optional hike, turn right and follow the spur trail to visit the small butte and granaries. Then return to the main path.

1.5 Arrive back at the trailhead.

26 Mesa Arch Trail

This short, easy hike takes you to spectacular Mesa Arch and an overlook above the Colorado River Canyon.

Distance: 0.5-mile loop
Approximate hiking time: 30 minutes
Difficulty: Easy; 100-foot elevation gain
Trail surface: Double-track dirt path
Best season: Year-round
Other trail users: None
Canine compatibility: No dogs allowed

Fees and permits: Daily fee to enter park
Maps: USGS Musselman Arch, *Moab Trails Illustrated Explorer*
Trail contacts: Canyonlands National Park, 2282 SW Resource Blvd., Moab 84532; (435) 719-2313 or for backcountry information (435) 259-4351; www.nps .gov/cany/index.htm

Finding the trailhead: From Moab, drive northwest on US 191 to UT 313. Turn left (south) on UT 313 and follow the paved road to Canyonlands National Park. From the visitor center, drive southwest 6.3 miles to the marked Mesa Arch parking area on the left (east) side of the road. GPS: N 38 23.348' / W 109 52.083'

The Hike

The short Mesa Arch Trail makes an open loop across the eastern edge of the Island in the Sky, a lofty mesa rimmed with vertical cliffs, ending at Mesa Arch and one of Canyonlands National Park's most dramatic scenic views. The wide, easy-to-follow trail, with a sand and slickrock surface, is marked by occasional cairns or rock piles and dried wood alongside it.

The trail ends abruptly at the unfenced edge of a 500-foot-high cliff below Mesa Arch. Watch your children

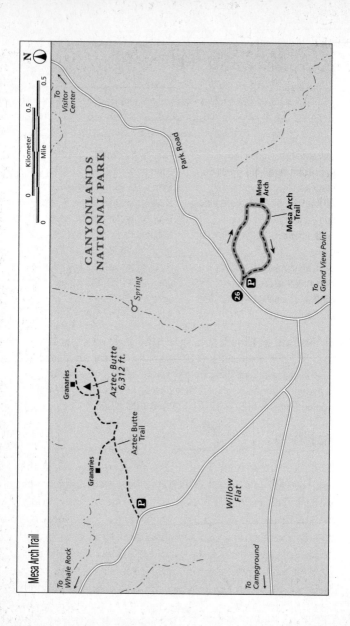

Mesa Arch Trail

CANYONLANDS NATIONAL PARK

To Whale Rock

Granaries

Granaries

Aztec Butte Trail

Aztec Butte
6,312 ft.

P

Willow Flat

To Campground

Spring

P

26

Mesa Arch

Mesa Arch Trail

To Grand View Point

Park Road

To Visitor Center

N

0   0.5
Kilometer

0   0.5
Mile

around the arch and don't step close to the edge since sandstone can crumble and break.

Start at the trailhead on the south side of the parking area and hike east. The trail forks after a few feet. Take the left fork. The sandy trail heads northeast across sandy soil studded with scattered juniper, piñon pine, and sagebrush. After reaching a slight rise, it descends down steps and slickrock to a trail junction just west of the arch. Go left and scramble up slickrock to Mesa Arch.

Mesa Arch, composed of Navajo Sandstone, is a cliff-hanging arch perched above a vertical 500-foot cliff of Wingate Sandstone. Below the arch and beyond the cliff edge is nothing but air. Mesa Arch is the most popular natural feature on the Island in the Sky, particularly for photographers who come at sunrise.

The wide view from Mesa Arch is simply spectacular. Precipitous cliffs line the Island's east side, towering above the White Rim and the hidden Colorado River canyon. Washer Woman Arch and neighboring Monster Tower stand apart from the rim and beyond rises blocky Airport Tower and the ragged outline of the La Sal Mountains over 35 miles to the northeast.

After enjoying the arch and the views, follow the trail back west 100 feet to a Y-junction. Take the left fork. The trail climbs up cross-bedded sandstone and stone steps to the crest of a low hill. Descend down lots of steps to the parking lot.

Miles and Directions

0.0 Begin at the trailhead.
0.25 Reach Mesa Arch.
0.5 Arrive back at the trailhead.

27 Upheaval Dome Overlook Trail

The trail leads to two overlooks on the south rim of spectacular Upheaval Dome, possibly a giant meteor crater, on the west side of the Island in the Sky.

Distance: 0.8 mile round trip to first overlook; 1.8 miles out and back to second overlook.

Approximate hiking time: 1 to 2 hours

Difficulty: Moderate; 150-foot elevation gain

Trail surface: Single-track dirt and slickrock trail

Best season: Year-round

Other trail users: None

Canine compatibility: No dogs allowed

Fees and permits: Daily fee to enter park

Maps: USGS Upheaval Dome, *Moab Trails Illustrated Explorer*

Trail contacts: Canyonlands National Park, 2282 SW Resource Blvd., Moab 84532; (435) 719-2313 or (435) 259-4351 for backcountry information; www.nps.gov/cany/index .htm

Finding the trailhead: From Moab, drive northwest on US 191 to UT 313. Turn left (south) on UT 313 and follow the paved road south to Canyonlands National Park. From the visitor center, drive southwest 6.5 miles to a junction with Upheaval Dome Road. Turn right and follow the Upheaval Dome Road for 4.8 miles to the Upheaval Dome parking lot and trailhead at the end of the road. GPS: N 38 25.577' / W 109 55.567'

The Hike

The Upheaval Dome Overlook Trail climbs to two different overlooks perched on the south side of Upheaval

Dome, one of the most dramatic natural features at Canyonlands National Park. Hikers can go to both overlooks for a 1.8-mile round-trip hike or just to the first overlook for a 0.8-mile hike. The trail is easy to follow, has generally low-angle grades, minimal elevation gain, and no drop-offs except at the fenced second overlook. Part of the second section of trail crosses slickrock pavement and is marked by cairns or rock piles.

Begin the hike at the trailhead at the end of the Upheaval Dome Road. There is usually plenty of parking except on busy days. A restroom and picnic tables are at the trailhead/parking area. From the trailhead sign, go right on the marked Upheaval Dome Overlook Trail.

Walk 0.1 mile on the trail to a junction with the Syncline Loop Trail, which makes an 8.3-mile loop around Upheaval Dome. Continue straight on the signed Upheaval Dome Overlook Trail.

The trail heads up a long series of stone steps to a rock-lined dirt path. A trail junction is reached at 0.4 mile from the trailhead. The left trail goes to the west overlook. Go straight for 150 feet onto a rounded sandstone dome that overlooks Upheaval Dome. A couple of interpretative signs explain two theories about how the dome formed.

Upheaval Dome is a bizarre geographic feature with upturned sandstone beds along its edges and a deep crater filled with multicolored sediments. The rock layers on the edge, composed of Wingate Sandstone and Kayenta Formation, are twisted, heaved, and uplifted into a circular crater almost 3 miles in diameter. Geologists have long thought that the feature was a collapsed salt dome that formed when salt flowed upward and pushed up the sandstone layers, which were later eroded into today's shape.

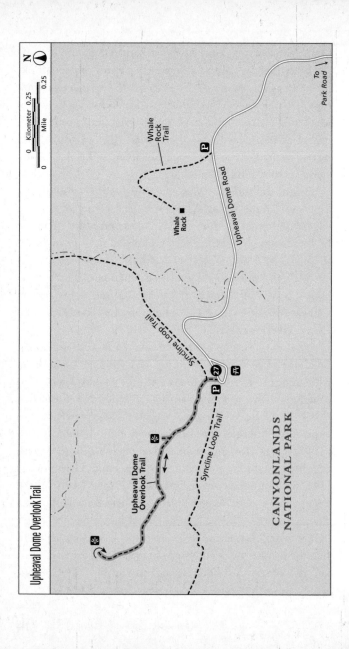

Upheaval Dome Overlook Trail

Whale Rock Trail

Whale Rock

Upheaval Dome Road

P

To Park Road

Syncline Loop Trail

27

P

Upheaval Dome Overlook Trail

Syncline Loop Trail

CANYONLANDS NATIONAL PARK

N

0   Kilometer   0.25
0   Mile   0.25

A newer theory is that Upheaval Dome is actually the impact crater of a meteorite that hit the earth between 60 and 160 million years ago. The meteorite, which was between 500 and 1,000 feet in diameter and traveling about 25,000 miles per hour, crashed into the ground, creating a huge explosion and the crater.

Most hikers go to this first overlook and then return back to the trailhead for a 0.8-mile round trip hike. But it's well worth the time and energy to hike another half mile out the trail to the second overlook for another spectacular view into Upheaval Dome.

From the first overlook, hike 150 feet back to the trail junction. If you want to return to the trailhead, go straight. To go to the second overlook, take a right on the marked trail. This second trail segment is 0.5 mile to the west, making it a 1-mile round-trip hike from the junction.

The dirt trail heads west alongside the sandstone rim of the dome and then descends down slickrock slabs to an old mining trail chiseled into a cliff. Descend the trail to a flat area and hike northwest to a fenced overlook behind a rock pillar. This dramatic viewpoint, perched on the edge of towering cliffs, looks directly down into the heart of Upheaval Dome. Keep an eye on children here and don't let them climb on the fence—it's a long way down to level ground.

After admiring the view, follow the trail back east for 0.5 mile to the trail junction at the first overlook, regaining 150 feet of elevation along the way. At the junction, go right and hike 0.4 mile downhill to the trailhead and the end of the hike.

Miles and Directions

0.0 Begin at the trailhead.

0.1 Reach a junction with Syncline Loop Trail. Go straight.

0.4 Come to a junction with a second overlook trail. Go straight 150 feet to the first overlook, then return to the junction and go right (east) to continue toward the second overlook.

0.9 Arrive at the second overlook. Begin retracing your steps to return.

1.4 Reach the junction at the first overlook. Go right.

1.8 Arrive back at the trailhead.

28 Whale Rock Trail

A fun easy hike up the rounded slickrock dome of Whale Rock offers panoramic views of the Island in the Sky, a narrow mesa lined with cliffs in the northern sector of Canyonlands National Park.

Distance: 0.8 mile out and back
Approximate hiking time: 30 minutes to 1 hour
Difficulty: Easy; 100-foot elevation gain
Trail surface: Dirt and slickrock trail
Best season: Year-round
Other trail users: None
Canine compatibility: No dogs allowed

Fees and permits: Daily fee to enter park
Maps: USGS Upheaval Dome, *Moab Trails Illustrated Explorer*
Trail contacts: Canyonlands National Park, 2282 SW Resource Blvd., Moab 84532; (435) 719-2313 or (435) 259-4351 for backcountry information; www.nps.gov/cany/index .htm

Finding the trailhead: From Moab, drive northwest on US 191 to UT 313. Turn left (south) on UT 313 and follow the paved road south to Canyonlands National Park. From the visitor center, drive southwest 6.5 miles to a junction with Upheaval Dome Road. Turn right and follow Upheaval Dome Road for 4.5 miles to the Whale Rock parking lot and trailhead on the right (north) side of the road. GPS: N 38 25.613' / W 109 54.840'

The Hike

The short Whale Rock Trail is a fun hike to the humped summit of Whale Rock, a giant whale-shaped sandstone bluff. It's good for kids, who can scramble up low-angle slabs on the summit ridge. Keep an eye on the youngsters

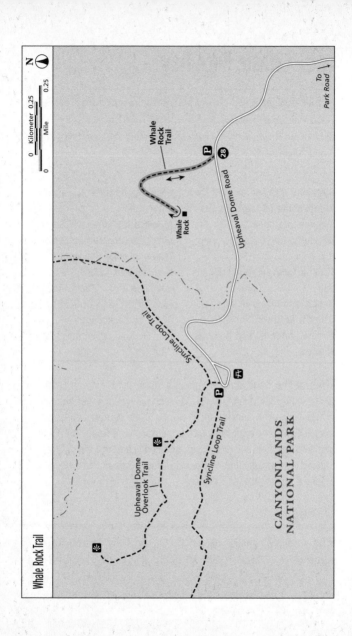

Whale Rock Trail

Whale Rock Trail

Whale Rock

Upheaval Dome Road

28

P

Syncline Loop Trail

Upheaval Dome
Overlook Trail

Syncline Loop Trail

P

CANYONLANDS
NATIONAL PARK

To
Park Road

N

0   Kilometer 0.25

0   Mile   0.25

though, since both sides of the ridge drop off steeply. The trail is easy to follow and well marked with cairns or stacks of stones.

Start at the trailhead on the west side of the parking area on Upheaval Dome Road. The wide trail heads north across sandy hummocks anchored with scattered juniper trees, piñon pine, and sagebrush and over open sandstone slabs. After 0.2 mile the trail begins ascending up slabs to Whale Rock's east ridge.

Walk up the broad ridge on solid bedrock sandstone. Whale Rock is composed of Navajo Sandstone, a widespread formation that was deposited as immense sand dunes about 170 million years ago. At the end of the hike you'll reach a final cap of broken rock. Scramble directly up to the summit, using big footholds.

You'll find expansive views on top. To the southeast rises the Aztec Butte, a flat-topped mesa. To the southwest is the precipitous west rim of the Island in the Sky, Candlestick Tower, and beyond spreads The Maze, a remote wilderness of canyons on the western edge of Canyonlands National Park.

For extra credit, scramble west down the whale's back and climb up to the blowhole and the lower west summit at the head. After admiring the views and having a drink of water, head back down the trail 0.4 mile to the trailhead.

Miles and Directions

0.0 Begin at the trailhead on Upheaval Dome Road.

0.2 Reach the base of the east ridge.

0.4 Arrive at Whale Rock's summit. Begin descent to return on same route.

0.8 Arrive back at the trailhead.

29 Grand View Point Trail

An easy hike along the airy rim at the southern tip of Canyonlands National Park's Island in the Sky plateau takes you to a lofty overlook.

Distance: 2 miles out and back
Approximate hiking time: 1 to 1½ hours
Difficulty: Easy; 50-foot elevation gain
Trail surface: Single- and double-track dirt and slickrock trail. First part of trail is concrete and wheelchair accessible.
Best season: Year-round
Other trail users: None
Canine compatibility: No dogs allowed
Fees and permits: Daily fee to enter park
Maps: USGS Monument Basin, *Moab Trails Illustrated Explorer*
Trail contacts: Canyonlands National Park, 2282 SW Resource Blvd., Moab 84532; (435) 719-2313 or (435) 259-4351 for backcountry information; www.nps.gov/cany/index.htm

Finding the trailhead: From Moab, drive northwest on US 191 to UT 313. Turn left (south) on UT 313 and follow the paved road south to Canyonlands National Park. From the visitor center, drive southwest 6.5 miles to a road junction. Keep left on the main road and drive another 6 miles to the end of the road and a large parking area. GPS: N 38 18.643' / W 109 51.394'

The Hike

The Grand View Point Trail, following first the eastern rim and then the western rim of the Island in the Sky is an easy hike that ends at an airy viewpoint near the southern tip of the Island. The trail is mostly flat, crossing expanses of slickrock pavement and dirt sections. It may be hard to follow in a couple of spots, but the trail is generously marked with cairns. The first 300 feet of the trail from the parking area to Grand View Point Overlook is a concrete sidewalk that is wheelchair accessible.

Be very careful and don't get too close to the cliff edge. The vertical Wingate sandstone cliffs below the rim are over 300 feet high and there are no safety fences either along the trail or at the ending overlook. Watch small children and don't let them venture close to the edge. In summer, bring water, sunscreen, and a hat. There is virtually no shade along the trail.

From the trailhead, walk 300 feet down the concrete trail to 6,080-foot Grand View Point Overlook. This spectacular fenced overlook offers dramatic views across Canyonlands National Park. Below is White Rim, a wide bench below the cliffs, and Monument Basin, a deep canyon studded with thin pinnacles including the slender Totem Pole. Beyond lies a maze of canyons that stretch to the Abajo Mountains on the horizon.

The trail heads south (right) from Grand View Overlook, descending stone steps to a wide bench formed from gray Kayenta sandstone. Hike south along the east rim on slickrock pavement, then climb stone steps to a dirt-trail section. An abrupt 300-foot drop-off is always to your left. After 0.6 mile the trail climbs away from the eastern rim and follows bedrock southwest across the top of the mesa and then descends stone steps to the western rim.

After a mile the trail ends near the abrupt end of the Island in the Sky at an unfenced overlook. New views of wild and remote country unfold south and west of the Island in the Sky, including the hidden canyon of the Green River, The Maze, the distant Orange Cliffs, and the Henry

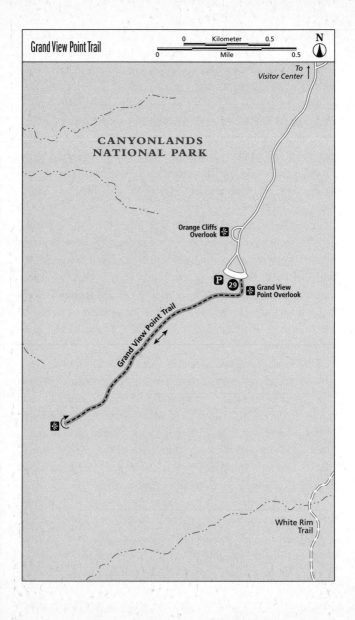

Grand View Point Trail

To
Visitor Center

CANYONLANDS
NATIONAL PARK

Orange Cliffs
Overlook

P 29 Grand View
Point Overlook

Grand View Point Trail

White Rim
Trail

N

Kilometer
0 0.5
Mile
0 0.5

Mountains, the last discovered and named mountain range in the lower forty-eight states. Directly south is Junction Butte, an isolated sky island. This is a perfect place to watch and photograph the sunset.

Finish the hike by retracing your route back to the trailhead.

Miles and Directions

0.0 Start at the trailhead on the east side of the lot. After walking 300 feet, arrive at the Grand View Point Overlook and the end of the concrete surface. Go right (south).

0.6 Leave the east rim and climb onto the top of the mesa.

1.0 End at the overlook at the tip of the mesa. Turn to retrace your route.

2.0 Arrive back at the trailhead.

Appendix

Hiking, Climbing, and Canyoneering Guide Services

Canyonlands Field Institute
1320 South US 191/P.O. Box 68
Moab, UT 84532
(435) 259-7750 or (800) 860-5262
www.canyonlandsfieldinst.org

Destination Moab
HC 64 Box 3214
Moab, UT 84532
(435) 259-4772
www.destinationmoab.com

Moab Adventure Center
225 South Main St.
Moab, UT 84532
(435) 259-7019 or (866) 904-1163
www.moabadventurecenter.com

Moab Cliffs and Canyons
253 North Main St.
Moab, UT 84532
(435) 259-3317 or (877) 641-5271
www.cliffsandcanyons.com

Moab Desert Adventures
415 North Main St.
Moab, UT 84532
(877) ROK-MOAB (765-6622) or (435) 260-2404
www.moabdesertadventures.com

Management Agencies

Arches National Park
P.O. Box 907
Moab, UT 84532
(435) 719-2299
www.nps.gov/arch/index.htm

Bureau of Land Management
Moab Field Office
82 East Dogwood
Moab, Utah 84532
(435) 259-2100
www.blm.gov/ut/st/en/fo/moab.html or www.blm.gov/
ut/st/en/fo/moab/recreation/campgrounds.html (camping
information)

Canyonlands National Park
2282 SW Resource Blvd.
Moab, Utah 84532
(435) 719-2313 or (435) 259-4351 (backcountry information)
www.nps.gov/cany/index.htm

Dead Horse Point State Park
P.O. Box 609
Moab, UT 84532-0609
(435) 259-2614
www.utah.com/stateparks/dead_horse.htm

Conservation Organization

Nature Conservancy, Moab Project Office
P.O. Box 1329/820 Kane Creek Blvd.
Moab, UT 84532
(435) 259-4629
http://www.nature.org/wherewework/northamerica/
states/utah/preserves/art5828

General Moab Information

www.moab.net
www.moab-utah.com
www.discovermoab.com
www.go-utah.com/Moab

Medical and Emergency Services

Allen Memorial Hospital
719 West 400 North
Moab, UT 84532
(435) 259-7191
www.amhmoab.org

Grand County Sheriff's Office
(435) 259-8115 or 911

Grand County Search and Rescue (GCSAR)
P.O. Box 1343
Moab, UT 84532
www.gcsar.org

About the Author

Stewart M. Green has been traveling to the Moab area to hike and climb for more than thirty years. He lives in Colorado Springs, Colorado, where he works as a freelance writer and photographer for FalconGuides/Globe Pequot Press. He's written over twenty travel and climbing books for Globe Pequot, including *KNACK Rock Climbing, Rock Climbing Colorado, Rock Climbing Europe, Rock Climbing Utah, Rock Climbing Arizona,* and *Rock Climbing New England*. Stewart, a lifelong climber, began his climbing career in Colorado at age twelve and has since climbed all over the world. He's also a professional climbing guide with Front Range Climbing Company and the About.com Guide to Climbing. Visit him at www.stewartgreen.com.